本研究为2016年国家留学基金阶段研究成果
本研究受到西北工业大学专著出版基金资助
本研究为西北工业大学高教研究基金阶段成果

On English Teacher Education of European and American Universities in Bologna Process

博洛尼亚进程的欧美大学英语教师教育研究

ZHAO SHUO

赵　硕◎著

中国社会科学出版社

图书在版编目(CIP)数据

博洛尼亚进程的欧美大学英语教师教育研究：英文/赵硕著．—北京：中国社会科学出版社，2016.8

ISBN 978－7－5161－9048－7

Ⅰ.①博… Ⅱ.①赵… Ⅲ.①英语—师资培养—研究—欧洲 ②英语—师资培养—研究—美国 Ⅳ.①H319

中国版本图书馆 CIP 数据核字(2016)第 237603 号

出 版 人　赵剑英
选题策划　郭　鹏
责任编辑　郭　鹏
责任校对　董晓月
责任印制　李寡寡

出　　版　中国社会科学出版社
社　　址　北京鼓楼西大街甲 158 号
邮　　编　100720
网　　址　http://www.csspw.cn
发 行 部　010－84083685
门 市 部　010－84029450
经　　销　新华书店及其他书店

印　　刷　北京明恒达印务有限公司
装　　订　廊坊市广阳区广增装订厂
版　　次　2016 年 8 月第 1 版
印　　次　2016 年 8 月第 1 次印刷

开　　本　710×1000　1/16
印　　张　14
字　　数　230 千字
定　　价　56.00 元

《博洛尼亚进程的欧美大学英语教师教育研究》
专著撰写组

负责人： 赵　硕

成　员： 王晓丹　栗　霞　赵欣怡

序　一

赵硕副教授在他的新作《博洛尼亚进程的欧美大学英语教师教育研究》即将付梓之际，邀我为该书写序。我和赵老师有师生之谊，又在见他近年来力作不断，就很高兴为他的新作写几句话。

经济全球化加速了教育国际化的进程。在世纪之交的 1999 年 29 个欧洲国家的教育部长在意大利的博洛尼亚大学签署了《博洛尼亚宣言》，成立了欧洲高等教育区，开启了欧洲高等教育国际化的进程。博洛尼亚进程开局良好，其后十年共有 46 个国家加入了这个行动计划，连大洋彼岸的美国对这项改革也给予极大的关注。

为了适应教育国际化需要，欧洲不少国家的高校逐步把教学语言改为英语。因此，在博洛尼亚进程中研究如何提高教师的英语授课水平和教学质量，是至关重要的。

赵硕老师的新作研究了博洛尼亚进程的欧美大学英语教师教育理论与现状，详细阐述了该进程对欧美大学英语教育的影响与变革，案例分析既有欧美公立大学英语教育模式，也有私立大学英语教育模式，同时阐述了欧美大学英语教师专业发展理论的现状。我通读全稿后，感触良多，该书有不少创新亮点，可归纳为以下三个方面：

一、在理论层面，这项研究从历时与共时两个维度梳理有关博洛尼亚进程的欧美大学英语教师教育体系，从欧美大学英语教师专业发展理论、合作教学、反思性教学、行动研究、教师信念、语料库教学、学术生态发展与学科创新能力等多角度来探讨欧美大学博洛尼亚进程十五年来英语教师教育发展的一般趋势，同时与我国公办与民办大学进行比较教育研究。

二、在实践层面，这本专著创新性地创建了英语教师教育发展的学习型组织，是这项研究在理论研究的基础上提出的旨在提高英语教师教育专业水平的实践性成果。详细分析了博洛尼亚进程的欧美大学语料库教学发展的新动态，案例分析选取了英国、美国、德国、瑞典、西班牙、芬兰等国的语料库教学模式；同时这本专著创新性地研究了欧美大学英语教师教育的生态发展理论，提出了大学英语教师教育的生态优化问题。

三、在应用层面，该专著在分析和研究博洛尼亚进程的欧美大学英语教师教育理论与现状基础上，详细提出了如何用新的教师教育发展理念和措施改善我国公办与民办大学英语教师教育的途径，借鉴欧美国家大学英语教师教育模式解读了我国高校英语教师教育发展的两种倾向："工具性专业发展"和"主体性专业发展"的现象，提出了我国大学英语教师教育的行动研究策略。

《博洛尼亚进程的欧美大学英语教师教育研究》的付梓又一次见证了赵硕副教授在外语教育领域的不懈探索和追求。我期待他不断有力作问世，使广大外语学界同人能从中获益。

戴炜栋

2016 年 5 月

于　上海外国语大学

序　二
Preface

Congratulation on the new book of Professor ZHAO SHUO. This book entitled "On English Teachers Education of European and American Universities in Bologna Process" conducts a detailed research on teacher education of European and American Universities along the Bologna Process. It discusses Bologna Process influence on European universities, which cites the case analysis of public universities and private universities in Europe. In addition the book introduces teacher education approaches in universities. From the theoretical perspective, the book analyzes the teacher education framework in Bologna Process, which involves teachers' professional development, collaborative teaching, reflective teaching, action research and corpus-based teacher training.

From a diachronic perspective, the book discusses the developing trends in European and American universities within fifteen years of Bologna Process, in which some universities in UK, U. S., Spain, Germany, Sweden and Finland arc analyzed in detail. Also, the book illustrates corpus-based teacher training model that reflects ICT-based education model in European universities (i. e. UB University of Barcelona). Further, the book puts forward the ideal of optimizing ecological teacher education and learning organization innovation in university teacher education.

Onthe basis of analysis and introduction to teachers' education of European and American Universities, the book analyzes the enlightenment and reference to Chinese public and private universities. Anyhow we have to admit that teacher education and exchange students have been emphasized and promoted since Bologna Process, in which some successful experiences are discussed and referred to China. Especially those with a close tie between Chinese universities and European universities, teacher contact and teacher exchange will be promoted in the near future.

The Bologna Process was a framework and a model for University reform. It was a collective effort promoted by the European Union aiming at setting the basis for the integration of the European education and training systems, and specifically making compatible with the university studies and the three-cycle system (bachelor/master/doctorate). This great effort demanded the close collaboration of the public authorities and universities, assuring quality in study plans and new careers. Now, as a consequence of this long process, the mobility of students and university lecturers beyond their national borders is a reality. In the same time, we hope that there will be more academic exchange between Chinese university teachers and European university teachers. The publication of the book will be beneficial to university teachers' education not only in China but in Europe. Hence it is very significant to publish the book.

Professor Mario Barajas Frutos

Universitat de Barcelona

马里奥·巴拉哈斯 教授

2016 年 5 月

于 西班牙巴塞罗那大学

序　三

Prefacio（西班牙语）

Felicidades por el nuevo libro del profesor Zhao Shuo. Este libro titulado "Investigación sobre La Educación de Los Profesores de Inglés de Universidades Europeas y Americanas en El Proceso de Bolonia" conduce una investigación detallada sobre la formación del profesorado de universidades Europeas y Americanas a lo largo del proceso de Bolonia. Trata de las influencias del proceso de Bolonia en las universidades europeas, cuyos ejemplos analizados incluyen tanto universidades públicas como privadas en Europa. Al mismo tiempo, el libro también presenta una metodología teórica sobre la formación del profesorado universitario. Desde la perspectiva teórica, el libro analiza el marco de desarrollo de la formación docente en el proceso de Bolonia, el cual involucra el desarrollo profesional de los profesores, enseñanza colaborativa, enseñanza reflexiva, investigación de operaciones y la formación del profesorado basada en corpus.

Desde una perspectiva diacrónica, el libro analiza las tendencias de desarrollo en universidades europeas y americanas dentro de quince años del proceso de Bolonia, en el cual algunas universidades de El Reino Unido, Los Estados Unidos de América, España, Alemania, Suecia y Finlandia son analizadas con detalle. Además, el libro ilustra detalladamente el modelo de formación docente basado en el corpus, analiza ICT-basado en modelo de educación en universidades europeas (el ejemplo escogido fue UB, Universitat de Barcelona). Adicionalmente, el libro propone el concepto de la educación ecológica que mejorar la formación del profesorado y la organización innovadora del aprendizaje.

Sobre la base del análisis y la introducción a la educación de las universidades europeas y americanas de los profesores, el libro analiza la inspiración y la referencia surgida de la formación docente del proceso de Bolonia para las universidades públicas y privadas de chinas. De todos modos, tenemos que admitir que la formación docente y el intercambio de estudiantes se han enfatizado y promovido desde el proceso de Bolonia, en el cual algunas experiencias exitosas deben ser consideradas en las universidades de china. Especialmente, debido a las relaciones cada vez más cerca entre universidades chinas y universidades europeas, los contactos e intercambios entre profesores serán promovidas en un futuro cercano.

El proceso de Bolonia era un marco y un modelo para la reforma universitaria. Fue un esfuerzo colectivo promovido por la Unión Europea con el objetivo de establecer las bases para la integración de los sistemas de educación y formación europeos, y en concreto haciendo compatible con los estudios universitarios y el sistema de tres ciclos (grado/posgrado/doctorado). Este gran esfuerzo exigió la estrecha colaboración de las autoridades públicas y las universidades, asegurando la calidad de los planes de estudio y nuevas carreras. Ahora, como consecuencia de este largo proceso, la movilidad de estudiantes y profesores universitarios más allá de sus fronteras nacionales es una realidad. Al mismo tiempo, también esperamos que habrá más intercambio académico entre profesores universitarios chinos y profesores universitarios europeos.

La publicación del libro será beneficiosa para la educación del profesorado universitario no solo en China, sino también en Europa. Por lo tanto, la publicación del libro será un acto significativo.

Professor Mario Barajas Frutos

Universitat de Barcelona

马里奥·巴拉哈斯 教授

2016 年 5 月

于　西班牙巴塞罗那大学

前　言

博洛尼亚进程以其丰富的内涵、统一性与一体化相结合的特点，为欧美高等教育的建设带来了广阔的人文背景，对欧美大学的改革带来了活力和动力，提高了欧美高等教育在国际市场的竞争力，提升了欧美大学创建世界一流大学的共同愿景。

从知识经济全球化信息化来看，博洛尼亚进程的欧美大学教师教育研究日益成为一种超越国家范畴的宏观教育模式，其研究成果可以为世界各国的大学教师教育提供借鉴。进入二十一世纪后中国高校教师教育现状，尤其是英语教师教育状况及其学术水平不容乐观，加强我国英语教师教育建设及英语教师教育理论研究已经成为刻不容缓的课题。尤其在当前我国高等教育改革正在深入推进的时机下，借鉴博洛尼亚进程的欧美大学英语教师教育模式、潜心学习并思考高校英语教师的专业自主发展模式以尽快适应当今国际高等教育一体化时代所赋予的使命显得尤为重要，这不仅体现了我国高校教师教育发展战略，更是我们长期从事英语教师教育工作者责无旁贷的使命。

本书研究了博洛尼亚进程的欧美大学英语教师教育的理论与现状，详细阐述了博洛尼亚进程对于欧美大学英语教育的影响与变革，案例分析既有欧美公立大学英语教育模式，也有私立大学英语教育模式，同时阐述了欧美大学英语教师专业发展现状。在理论和实践层面主要包括以下内容：(1) 在理论层面，本研究从历时与共时两个维度梳理了有关博洛尼亚进程的欧美大学英语教师教育体系，从欧美大学英语教师专业发展理论、合作教学、反思性教学、行动研究、教师信念、语料库教学、学术生态发展与学科创新能力等多角度来探讨欧美大学博洛尼亚进程十五年来英语教师教育发展的一般趋势，同时与我国公办与民办大学进行比较教育研究；(2) 在实践层面，本专著创新性地创建了英语教师教育发展的学习型组织，在理论研究的基础上提出了旨在提高英语教师教育专业发展的实践性成果。同时详细分析了博洛尼亚进程的欧美大学语料库教学发展的新动态和对大学教师教育的促进作用，案例分析选取了英国、美国、德国、瑞典、西班牙、芬兰等国大学的英语教师教育模式。在此基础上本专著创新性地研究了欧美大学英语教师教育的生态发展理论，提出了大学英语教师教育的生态优化问题。

本专著包括七章内容，从博洛尼亚进程十五年来欧美大学英语教师教育发展现状出发，介绍了 ELT（英语教师教育）在欧美大学的应用与发展，研究了欧美大学英语教师专业发展理论、合作教学、反思性教学、行动研究、教师信念、语料库教学、学术生态发展与学科创新能力等英语教师教育模式，最后从理论与实践结合的角度讨论了博洛尼亚进程十五年来欧美大学英语教师教育发展对我国大学英语教师的启示与借鉴，提出了我国公办与民办高校英语教师教育自主发展策略。

本书在分析和研究博洛尼亚进程的欧美大学英语教师教育理论与现状基础上，详细提出了如何用新的教师教育发展理念和措施改善我国公办与民办大学英语教师教育的途径，如何借鉴欧美国家大学英语教师教育模式来解读我国高校英语教师教育发展的两种倾向："工具性专业发展"和"主体性专业发展"的现象，提出了我国大学英语教师教育的行动研究策略。以博洛尼亚进程十五年来欧美大学高等教育发展为参照维度，将十五年来欧美大学英语教师教育发展划分为不同阶段进行梳理，透过繁杂的史实资料捕捉欧美大学英语教师教育由"工具性专业发展"向"主体性专业发展"进步的历史轨迹。

笔者长期从事博洛尼亚进程的欧美大学教育研究，积累了一定数量的第一手资料，总结出博洛尼亚进程十五年来相当数量的欧美大学教师教育的变革案例。同时笔者先后在瑞典、西班牙、葡萄牙、法国、德国、奥地利、匈牙利、捷克、波兰、芬兰和美国等博洛尼亚进程国进行过实地调研，积累了一定数量的第一手资料。但是笔者并不奢望依赖自己已掌握的知识信息与有限的经验去建立一个系统而全面的理论框架和实践模型，而是希望凭借撰写者的努力和心血力图传递一些建设性信息，以激发他人做更高层次上的批判性思考和探究。

本书的中文序言由上海外国语大学的戴炜栋教授撰写，戴教授是我国著名的外语教育学家、上海外国语大学前任校长，也是我在上海外国语大学攻读博士的导师，是我十分敬重的良师益友。戴教授十分关心我的个人成长，每当我取得一点小小的进步戴教授总是给予我亲切的支持和鼓励，使我受益匪浅。当本书即将完稿之际，我在西班牙巴塞罗那大学请戴炜栋教授为本书作序时，戴教授在仔细了解了书稿内容后对笔者的研究工作给予了肯定，并慨然应允作序，对此笔者深表感谢。

本书的英文和西班牙语序言由西班牙巴塞罗那大学的 Mario Barajas 教授撰写，Mario Barajas 教授是巴塞罗那、加泰罗尼亚以及西班牙著名的高等教育学专家，长期从事博洛尼亚进程的欧美大学现代信息技术发展与教师教育研究，有着丰富的教师教育研究经验。同时 Mario Barajas 教授也是笔者在西班牙巴塞罗那大学做博士后研究的合作教授与合作导师之一，对笔者在巴塞罗那大学的研究工作给予了大量的帮助。

本书的撰写和修订工作经历了近两年时间，融入了本书研究人员大量的心血与努力。当我正在考虑如何进一步了解美国高校英语教师教育的现状时，笔者的同事晓丹老师曾在美国堪萨斯 JCCC 学院做过英语教学工作，她在美国的教学实践和调研充实了博洛尼亚进程在美国高校英语教师教育的案例分析，对此我深表感谢。在此还要感谢葡萄牙里斯本大学 Ricardo Reis 先生、Cláudia Duarte 女士，意大利博洛尼亚大学 Celeste Messina 女士，西班牙庞培法布拉大学谢峰博士、袁陈杰博士，西班牙格拉纳达大学张雅妮硕士，西班牙国家量子科学研究所冉仕举博士后，法国里尔大学林天骏博士，意大利佛罗伦萨大学美术学院袁之雅硕士等（这里我就不再一一列举），我在巴塞罗那、塞维利亚、格拉纳达、萨拉戈萨、巴伦西亚、里斯本、波尔图、蒙彼利埃、图卢兹、马赛、摩纳哥、布拉格、华沙、佛罗伦萨和博洛尼亚等大学调研欧洲大学教师教育时得到了他们的大力支持，了解到许多宝贵的信息，对此我深表谢意。此外我还想借此机会感谢我的邻居巴塞罗那大学的双学士王莉同学，我在访谈时她给我提出了很多建设性的意见，王莉从小在西班牙 Mallorca（马洛卡群岛）长大，西班牙语几乎就是她的母语，她对西班牙大学教育的见解和独立自主的生活能力给我留下了深刻的记忆。

本书的读者对象包括英语语言学和教育学专业的本科、硕士和博士研究生，同时也是其它相关学科研究欧美大学教师教育可供借鉴的书籍，也可以用于国外大学二语习得和教师教育培训的教材和专门书籍。

最后，笔者引用彼得·圣吉（P. M. Senge）博士在《第五项修炼》

书中的一段话借以自勉，以鼓励自己和他人去开拓研究博洛尼亚进程的欧美大学教师教育新乐园。“你明白自己的任何‘答案’，充其量不过是‘近似值’，总还有改善的余地。你可能不断在磨练自己解决问题的理性能力，并在过程中将这项能力尽量发挥，而一直都知道这还是不够的。”

赵硕

2016 年 8 月

于　西班牙巴塞罗那大学

Contents

Chapter One Study of Education Theory and Its Relevance to Teacher Education

Speaking of education policy and theory, the Bologna Process is one of important reforms in education history. The Bologna Process is a series of ministerial meetings and agreements between European countries designed to ensure comparability in the standard and quality of higher education qualifications. Through Bologna Accords, the process has created European Higher Education Area, in particular under the Lisbon Recognition Convention.

It is named after the place it was proposed, the University of Bologna, with the signing of the Bologna declaration by Education Ministers from 29 European countries in 1999, forming a part of European integration. It was opened up to other countries signatory to the European Cultural convention of the Council of Europe; further governmental meetings have been held in Prague (2001), Berlin (2003), Bergen (2005), London (2007), and Leuven (2009). Prior to the signing of the Bologna declaration, the Magna Charta Universitatum (《欧洲大学宪章》) had been issued at a meeting of university rectors celebrating the 900th anniversary of the University of Bologna, and thus of European universities in 1998. One year before the Bologna declaration education ministers Claude Allegre (France), Jürgen Rüttgers (Germany), Luigi Berlinguer (Italy) and Baroness Blackstone (UK) signed the Sorbonne declaration in Paris in 1998, committing themselves to "harmonize the architecture of the European Higher Education system". The Bologna Process currently has 46 participating countries and 49 signatories.

1 – 1　**Bologna Process Conference**

1 – 2　**Sorbonne Declaration**

With the development of society, economy and people's ideology, English teachers' self-education ability and their education behavior start to develop, which is the maxim expectation of entire society on contemporary English teachers based on this. A new subject in Teachers' development as the research of teachers' professional development aims at the English teachers' professional development, psychological maturity and education theory formation to substantive discussion. From the development of English teachers' educational philosophy view, every teacher occupation development is accompanied by the whole process of growth and development of teachers by constantly improving, correction and internalization practice, which have gradually been formed. English teacher occupation development should have continued with extensibility features. English teaching and teachers' self development research and practice work has achieved certain results in European and American Universities since Bologna Process, but there are still some problems to be solved. For example the English teachers' education is also a lack of in-depth concrete and effective study, the unreasonable structure of the curriculum, the lack of targeting, professional and practical features. On the other hand, because of human resources, material energy and other factors, English teachers who pay attention to personal career development are less engaged in the work of teaching research, which is obvious at present. From the perspective of teaching reform modern education theory and ICT technology are not combined with their research work. With lack of self-reflection, self-observation and self-assessment, they cannot meet the requirements of modern English teaching.

In order to adapt to the development of English teaching situation, whether it's English teaching system (education policy, such as English learning system, the requirement of teacher professionalization) or from English teacher's self-developing ability and teaching education views (teaching program, teaching strategies, classroom teaching, classroom communication monitoring, teaching evaluation etc.), teacher education reform and development need to be done. However it does not raise teachers' dominant position and give play to teacher's personality characteristics before Bologna Process, then we have to say that such development is invalid and meaningless. Based on above points in this aspect, the author will then discuss English teacher education policy in Europe and America in order to introduce some precious experiences to give enlightenment to English teacher education development in China.

1.1 Teacher Education Policy in Europe and America

There are many famous universities in Europe and America, which is closely related to their teacher education policy. They are dominant representation in education in that studying the education policy in Europe and America has great meaning for other countries.

The EU started relatively late in the area of teacher education policy, but there are still some achievements that have positive effect on EU itself and its member states in teacher education policy and its practice. English teaching education policy mainly includes building a common standard, improving the quality of teacher education, promoting teachers' in-service professional development, perfecting the mechanism of teachers' team construction and so on. At present the focal point of the teacher education policy is to deepen teacher education policy dialogue mechanism, realize the integration of teacher education, build the index system of teacher education and teacher educators' ability and standard etc.

The policy content in Europe and America after Bologna Process can be summarized as: (1) Common standard of teachers, teachers' ability and qualification for the European union to provide a standardized reference; (2) Improving the quality of teacher education and highlighting the EU and its member states to higher quality education demands; (3) Promoting teachers' professional development in the EU and its member states and understanding teachers' career development; (4) Improving the mechanism of teachers' team construction and education development for the EU and its member states to provide a steady stream of power.

1.1.1 Building Mutual Teacher Standard

In order to guarantee teachers' ability and qualification of comparability, the European commission, which discussed teachers' ability and qualification in 2005, issued Common European Standard for Teacher Competence and Qualifications (hereinafter referred to as the "European Standard"), elaborating the common ability and qualification for European teachers. European Standard is mainly composed of common principles, key ability and policy suggestion of three parts. Common principles include high quality teachers' team, lifelong learning career, and flow of professional and cooperative ability.

The key ability involves collaboration with others, the ability to control knowledge, skills and information, ability to integrate into the community. Policy recommendations put forward that there should be high quality teachers in teams. Teachers should be the development of pre-service, induction and in-service professional development at a coherent phase. To encourage teachers' flow universities should pay attention to the participation of all stakeholders in the process of teacher training. In terms of common principles, high-quality teachers refer to such teachers as being able to develop by institutions of higher education. Teachers not only need to have a wide range of subject knowledge, they should also have knowledge of teaching and learning, guiding students' ability of learning and understanding the cause of education as well as its social and cultural dimensions.

The career of lifelong learning refers to the institutions attaching great importance to the concept of life-long study in the teachers' professional implement, providing opportunities for teachers' in-service professional development. At the same time teachers should be encouraged to participate in creative activities and scientific research activities in order to ensure that the pace of knowledge updates with the pace of social development. Professional flow refers to encouraging pre-service teacher education and in-service professional development phases so that teachers should actively participate in European project.

These projects provide the opportunities for teachers to work and study in other countries and improve the quality of teacher education and in-service professional development. Professional cooperation refers to the cultivation of teachers, such as in-service teacher education before stage as higher education institutions need to match with all interested partners to ensure the high quality teacher training in addition to higher education teaching agency, local governments, departments and other relevant institutions in cooperation. As to key ability, it refers to the ability to collaborate with others here "others" refers to the other main body of education environment, such as the individual students, teachers, individual and group.

Emphasis on teacher's ability to collaborate with others is to develop the learner's potential to help learners acquire the ability of collaboration with others. The ability of knowledge control, skills and information mainly refers to strengthening teachers'reflections on knowledge acquisition, analysis and transformation ability. Integrated into the society mainly refers to the ability of teachers in training learners' consciousness of social integration which plays an important role. As a result English teachers will be trained by promoting education flow between Europe and cross-cultural understanding in order to help students to cultivate the consciousness of European citizens and global citizen consciousness, which is able to help students understand the cultural diversity. In addition teachers themselves should move to integrate with local community in teacher education institutions, such as ability to cooperate with colleagues.

1.1.2 Improving Teacher Education Quality

The European Union recognizes that the quality of teaching level not only affects the quality of education and long-term competitiveness in Europe, but also it will produce important influence on target eventually. And the quality of teachers and quality of teacher education is one of the crucial links hence the EU increases much attention to English teacher education after Bologna Process.

As the change of times, English teachers not only spread knowledge and professional skills but they are leaders to help students'potential development and various abilities to become a qualified citizen in society. Therefore the original teacher education needs to be reformed in that the focus of reform lies in the promotion of teacher education quality.

On December 12, 2007, the EU formally released Conclusions of the-Council and the Representatives of the Governments of the Member States Meeting in order to improve the quality of teacher education and ensure the legitimacy of the policy and the effectiveness of implementation.

This file is mainly around the EU member states on the quality of teacher education, aiming at solving present quality problems of teacher education and putting forward policy suggestions. The file matched with teachers' education quality improvement policy which contains ensuring university teacher education, education theory and teaching practice of in-service teacher education curriculum before reasonable proportion so as to increase education skills in teachers' knowledge structure and the balance of specialized subject knowledge, providing vocational education for new teachers and teacher professional development to promote coherence. At the same time the development of teachers' leadership and management ability is to guarantee the quality of pre-service teacher education and in-service teacher professional development activities. Of course the purpose is to strengthen training teachers in the link to form a "learning community" in providing professional support to university teacher education and promoting the flow of each stage of teachers to stimulate teacher education and teaching activities in European dimension.

1.1.3 Promoting Teachers' In-service Professional Development

The teacher education policy set by the European Union has a larger part of policies which aims at professional development because the pre-service teacher education mainly involves the education sovereignty of EU member states.

At present EU aims at in-service teachers' professional development platform which has been gradually established, such as "Comenius, Basic Education Teachers Flow Plan", "In-service Teacher Professional Development Plan", "Erasmus Higher Education Teachers Flow Plan" etc. By encouraging teachers to participate in "Comenius, Basic Education Teachers Flow Plan", it can not only make teachers to learn new teaching methods and knowledge, but also promote their professional development in English teaching.

"Comenius, In-service Teacher Professional Development Plan" mainly adopts modern information communication technology (ICT) and method of network platform to build virtual community in in-service professional development for English teachers hence teachers' participation in virtual community realizes in-service professional development of all kinds of activities.

In order to further ensure members of the importance of teachers' professional development activities and formulate the corresponding teacher professional development policies, Council of the European Union specially issued the professional development of teachers and policy documents on June 2009, which made the member states and the European Union commit to the development of teachers education activities in specific provision.

Council Conclusions on Professional Development of Teachers was issued to support teachers'professional development in European Union, which is an important policy text on November 2009. The file points out that the current countries should provide teachers with a number of in-service professional development projects, and these projects are not limited to teacher's individual demand and the problems they are faced with in order to develop English teacher education.

Therefore each member state needs to increase the number of teachers'in-service professional development project at the same time and ensure that the content of in-service professional development programs is fully tied to needs of teachers and teaching practice so as to guarantee the quality development of teachers'in-service professional program. Hence the file also encourages teachers to participate in the activities of advanced professional training and teaching research projects to make full use of the opportunity to increase understanding of other disciplines and interdisciplinary abilities.

The file puts forward two levels separately in the European Union to illustrate function of university leaders and teachers in professional development activities in addition to professional development advice. Specifically the council points out that knowledge, skills and teacher competences are the most important factors affecting teacher education quality, teaching quality and teaching ability development when university teachers acquire their potential development in the future since present development of teachers is different from the past. The EU and its member states need to improve the perspective of lifelong development and professional development. As a result English teachers should give importance to it in their professional development.

1.1.4 Improving Construction Mechanism of Teacher Team

In view of current shortage of English teachers in EU, teacher profession becomes less attractive in universities. European commission issued a work report named Rethinking Education on November 2012 accordingly. Investing skills for better socio-economic outcomes to the problem of teachers' team construction has been implemented on deep discussion. According to the report, university teachers from different level of education system all over the world have important relationship with quality of teacher education. If teachers come from low level education, the more improvement of teacher education is necessary accordingly. Based on it, the European commission proposes some policy suggestions to improve teachers' professional appeal so that the construction mechanism of teacher team will be perfected gradually.

These Suggestions include ensuring teachers' professional status, making teachers the consensus of individual competence, improving teachers' professional treatment, implementing strict standard in university teacher selection in that it will broaden university teachers'developing prospects and give teachers more autonomy and expansion roles.

EU ensures that teachers' professional status refers to the stability of their profession, such as protecting rights of teachers' career. Moreover part of the EU countries perceives teachers as "civil servants" identity which helps ensure their professional status and extra professional rights, such as stable job and good welfare treatment so as to improve teachers'professional appeal.

In addition English teacher occupation is not usually considered to have strong professionalism in some EU countries so it leads to teacher's professional status to be lower, which limits more high-quality talents choose English teacher as a career. Because of this reason, the European commission proposes to deeply realize the professionalism of English teachers, enhance English teachers' professional recognition and professional specialization.

Anyhow the construction mechanism of teacher team will be improved in the following factors. First promotion of teacher's professional treatment and their economic perspective will provide more generous treatment for teachers. At present university teachers' payment is relatively low in many EU countries. Second implementation of strict teachers' selection and admittance mechanism will select highly qualified talents to join university teacher team. Third expanding teachers' career development prospect and providing diversified development prospect for teachers will be beneficial to teacher team construction, such as the diversification of teaching certification, a variety of in-service professional development programs, opportunity to study for a master and doctoral degree and so on. At last expanding the role of teachers' ability to fully understand their tasks will create opportunities for teachers to play initiatives, such as undertaking task in training and in-service teacher professional project, independent research project as well teaching, learning and scientific research etc. The purpose is to fully arouse the enthusiasm of teachers, extend teachers' roles and improve teachers' professional appeal.

1.2 English Education Theory in European and American Universities

The next discussion will be focused on how European countries and America implement these ideas and what kinds of contents and models are related in Bologna Process after general study of education policy in Europe and America.

1.2.1 Teacher Education in the United States

Before Bologna Process and European higher education development, European universities show lack of competitiveness because many of European students choose to study in the United States since 1990s. Therefore in the early stages of the Bologna Process the United States is once believed that this process is to aim at the development of higher education both in the United States and European countries, which continues to promote the progress of American higher education. But as European Higher Education Area (EHEA) gradually develops, American attitudes towards the Bologna Process have been obviously changed.

American higher education sectors begin to think more about international competitive level, education cooperation and practical education problems in the US and Europe than ever before. In order to deal with the Bologna Process the United States adopts a series of activities in different levels of higher education to promote the development of higher education in the United States. Official U. S. Education certification committee ACE (American Council on Education) starts to supervise the development of higher Education through the issuance of the international commission which is related to Bologna Process in U. S.

1 - 3 **Bologna Process in America**

1 - 4 **Exchange Students in USA**

Council of Graduate School of the United States is against Bologna Process in recent years and the Graduate School Council Conference adopts a three-year graduate degree. In addition, under the auspices of the Council of Graduate

School American universities also hold a "global strategic leadership with graduate education summit". Graduate education scholars from Europe, Australia, Canada, China and the United States gather together to discuss the future of postgraduate training mode in order to strengthen cooperation and jointly promote the development of master and doctorate education. The summit not only strengthens international cooperation in the countries of graduate education, but also stresses the competitive environment, which brought more international dialogue and cooperation for postgraduate education need.

The most important step in the United States in response to the Bologna process is the deepest concern on the international education organization, namely Association of International Educators (NAFSA), which specializes in the Bologna process-related activities. The working group provides the guiding principles for American higher education institutions to help teachers respond to changes in European higher education and promote dialogue between various American universities to provide comprehensive information. Many universities are informed decisions based on their specific circumstances and choices. As a regional advisory and information department, the working group in different universities not only introduces the procedure of the statute, but also holds seminars with the European Association of International Education (EAIE) together with discussion on the Bologna process.

Through continuous efforts the working group is also aware of the potential impact of European Higher Education Area in the US education system, such as unified degree system and mobility of students, but it is realized that the American educational institutions should be open-minded to seize the opportunity to cooperate with European Higher Education and strengthen each other in higher education qualifications, expand exchange and collaboration to abandon the concept of competition, as a result the Bologna Process accelerates mutual exchange of university students.

As can be seen from the above information, the United States starts to concern the Bologna process in the U. S as European higher education product in the United States is paid more attentions with the Bologna Process. American universities begin to change timely adjustment to the Bologna Process education.

At the same time American and European countries strengthen cooperation in higher education so that the United States can continue to promote the development of their higher education in the Bologna process.

1.2.2 Teacher Education in UK

Due to the Bologna Process influence in Europe, a growing number of British universities begin to develop the European strategy. British Institute of Higher Education implements the UK higher education policy assessment of credit accumulation and conversion of existing credit transfer system in the United Kingdom under the background of building European Higher Education Area on January 2013. Assessment study focuses on three issues: European Credit Accumulation and Transfer System (ECTS) in the implementation of the United Kingdom and teachers'devotion in teaching and learning process.

Credit refers to the different components of a course. After the completion of a degree it usually takes a certain number of credits to be obtained. The quality and quantity of learning credits include two value systems, hereby the general characteristics under study implies a certain level of quality that is achieved in learning outcomes and associated with the degree of complexity of knowledge. Hence teaching intelligence requires level, depth and breadth of learning. In general the British universities implements credit philosophy to cultivate independent learning ability of individual students and lifelong learning, highlight the role of credit-oriented features and incentives, emphasize student learning objectives and hobby-related use.

(1) Credit and Qualification Framework

UK has two higher degree qualification framework. The Framework for Higher Education Qualification hereinafter refers to FHEQ-WNI. The Framework for Qualifications of Higher Education in England, Scotland (SCQF), Wales and Northern Ireland is divided into three levels of higher education qualification framework for undergraduate and two graduate levels. They are individually Certificate Level, Intermediate Level, Honors Level, Master Level and Doctoral Level.

The first level of higher education qualification issues higher education certificate called Certificate of Higher Education, whose professional qualification is equivalent of a college matriculation. Intermediate includes ordinary (Honors), foundation degrees, higher education diploma. Honors degree in higher education is flexible in study, the general three-year and full-time course (some professions require four years) to get (Honors) Bachelor of Arts or Science. Masters have courses and academic year based on curriculum requirements, the degree is called MSC; academic master requires completing some research, the degree is called MPHiI. PhD (Doctorate Degree) is generally full-time for three years, mainly to original type of research-based Doctor of Philosophy (PhD) and another degree in related disciplines, including knowledge of research and study to obtain a professional name (Doctor of Education, EdD). Overall the UK degree in higher education system is based on three-tier framework, 3 – 4 years Bachelor, 1 – 2 years Master, 3 years PhD, which is consistent with the European Qualification Framework for Higher Education Area.

Steering Group of Measuring and Recording Student Achievement releases the Burgess Report in 2006, which starts at first in England, Scotland and wales together to build a unified framework, a credit system compatible with European credit. At the same time the British vocational education and trainers formulate a set of Qualifications and Credit Framework (QCF). Since 2008 the formal implementation helps realize different Qualifications and credits'accumulation and transformation between the degree-awarding institutions.

It is important to understand the vocational education qualification and credit framework and the connection between higher education credit framework and teacher education. UK Higher Education unites with BBS (The Forum for Bulletin Board System) to make a general principle with operating standard to help English teacher education qualification for further chances of teaching exchange students. Credit framework is consistent with UK higher education qualification framework and European higher education area qualification framework, namely ECTS credits = 2 England/Scotland/wales credits, hereby English teacher task is emphasized to help exchanged students acquire ECTS credits in UK.

(2) Teacher Education System in UK

British university will transfer credits through the equivalent treatment or "that" previous learning. Hence British Qualifications and Curriculum Development Agency (QCDA) issue teachers' standards to guide teachers in the following six steps on how to improve students' access to credit information consciousness, information collection and evaluation, evaluation and filing, feedback, credits grant and appeal. Generally the British universities will recognize learning component and previous learning method, hence pronounce differences in teachers' function. When applying for a professional teacher in British higher education entrance qualification, teachers learn that previous experience will not exert in present situation. Naturally many college and university teachers think there are many similar restrictions on their self-development.

British university curriculum requires basic task in teachers' education to form modularization and the biggest characteristic of modular curriculum is curriculum structure with relative independence, which separates the inspection of the comprehensive skills of course content in order to ensure that the quality of training can avoid learning content repetition, effectively reduce the learning load in classroom teaching. When using modular curriculum in widely available courses interdisciplinary ability of English teachers are urgently required according to course selection, cultivation of students' personality and ability.

In the practical management, many English teachers adopt flexible teaching skills to suit to ECTS characteristic and learning process. The demand for diversification and individuation of higher education choice really sets up the humanist education idea. Besides teacher education still emphasizes the effectiveness of the reasonable allocation of teacher resources to meet Bologna Process in UK.

1.2.3 Teacher Education in Germany

Germany is a signatory to the first batch of "Bologna Declaration" and also the active promoter in Bologna Process. The Bologna Process is the most extensive and most profound higher education reform in Germany in recent years, the main measures include:

(1) System of Higher Education Degree in Three Levels

The traditional academic degree system in Germany is the secondary academic degree system. The first level degree is divided into three types: Diploma (普通大学文凭), Magister (文科文凭) and Staat sexamen (国家专业考试文凭). Natural science, engineering science, social science and economics are generally granted Diploma degree, the humanities and social science are awarded the Magister degree, normal, medicine and law graduates will take part in the Staat sexamen. Hence the second level degree is PhD degree.

The first level degree according to different rules in the professional educational system is ranging from 4 to 6 years, normally university study lasts 5 years, applied sciences (FH) in university is for four years. The actual period of university study is an average of 4. 6 years and 6. 8 years. Traditional secondary degree system compared with the international mainstream bachelor and master on a tertiary degree system is not compatible. PhD students' learning achievements in Germany has difficulty to assess and recognize on the basis of international degree. At the same time benefits from German higher education become a big problem, which is both wasting of the limited education resources and affecting students' employment before Bologna Process.

In order to solve the above problems the 1998 revision of the structure of higher education law is allowed in the traditional academic degree system in colleges and universities correspondingly. Under the impetus of the Bologna process Germany revised the relevant provisions once again in 2002, the structure of higher education act includes the bachelor, master degree in professional settings to reach an agreement in 2010 to complete the reform of the academic degree system.

To the winter semester of 2006/07 there are a total of 11,492 professional teachers in Germany, of whom 45% has acquired master and PhD degree accordingly. Teachers' degree with international standards can be recognized easily, which strengthens the mobility of teachers.

At the same time the introduction of a master's degree in bachelor effectively shortens students'period to get a first class degree in the length of study, and also provides more opportunities for students to further studies. In order to improve international transparency of teachers' qualification in higher education and promote mutual recognition and understanding of exchange students, German universities introduce the Diploma Supplement to teachers. Diploma supplement is the attached file of higher education diploma, learning content, professional characteristics, diploma level and system of higher education in the country and it has been carried on the detailed instructions. In 2006 summer semester 63% of professional teachers obtained diploma supplement, which is a part of the first "Teacher Qualification Framework".

The framework regulation is issued by German higher education system in all kinds of diploma to guarantee teachers' qualification system description, including university teachers' general description, academic ability and quality description to adapt to ECTS learning quantity and admission standards. The framework is designed to improve the transparency of teachers' qualifications so that German universities will choose and employ English teachers easily. In addition the basis for teaching assessment and certification is listed. The traditional teaching method is adjusted to students' learning, teaching capacity, the new evaluation method and guidance to students' output orientation and transformation.

(2) European Credit Transfer System

The European credit transfer system (ECTS) is one of the credits in EU member states in the colleges and universities in the mutual recognition and conversion system, which is developed by the European commission and aims to provide a measurement, comparison and transformation between the college academic performances. This evaluation system has made a clear requirement to learning content and measurement, but not unified in comparable quantitative rules. European credit transfer system (ECTS) strengthens teachers' intensity in teaching and training. According to the prescribed length of teaching ECTS needs at least 100 credit hours to finish a bachelor course.

However the introduction of the credit system better solves the following problems: first students' learning pressure is effectively eased and students' learning burden is released; second the system's evaluation time includes both classroom learning time and the time needed for students' knowledge seeking, which is guided by teachers in learning so as to fully mobilize the students' learning enthusiasm and initiative and effectively develops the students' self-study ability; third as for teaching requirements it will thus effectively improve students' flexibility and mobility; fourth students will also get a relative performance level except for domestic universities evaluation scores. Accordingly the relative performance is divided into five evaluation levels based on academic achievement of teachers' recognition.

(3) Improving Teacher Education Quality Assurance

German higher education structure method specifies teaching, scientific research and talents training. Students must participate in the evaluation of teaching quality in colleges and universities, the assessment should be officially announced. Federal state law of higher education on the basis of the appraisal method and appraisal institution is further defined as evaluation period. In 1998 the federal government and state governments jointly launched the "Q" project since the project aims to improve different methods of quality assurance and coordination of German teachers in the whole European quality assurance system. Until 2013 the federal government's appropriation measures more than 50 million euros a year in project implementation.

Teacher quality assurance system is mainly composed of professional certification and the teaching evaluation to ensure a bachelor degree and master degree in professional teaching quality and uniform standard. In 1999 Germany set up Akkreditierungsrat (德国大学教师认证委员会), which is a professional certification committee and is responsible for Akkreditierungsagenturen to supervise their certification. German professional certification committee and all kinds of professional certification are institution bodies of international teacher education quality assurance association, the European association of higher education quality assurance (QA). In principle all the new professional teachers go through professional certification, and should be certified every five years. The whole certification process includes choosing professional certification institution and signing agreement, together with providing self-assessment report, professional certification assessment and decision feedback. The evaluation on teachers is made every five years, which includes department self-assessment, evaluation group evaluation and conclusion report. Department report should be submitted to the final evaluation in universities.

Teacher Evaluation mainly relates to the professional teaching conditions, teaching content, teaching management, teaching process, employment and professional advantages, weakness and characteristic analysis. At present German universities has established Evaluations Agent Union that is responsible for the implementation of teachers evaluation.

(4) Promoting International Flow of Teachers

The federal government amended the education to promote teachers reform act to encourage university courses in the internationalization of a series of English teaching and attract more foreign students to study in Germany. In addition the federal government launched a series of promoting the international movement of student projects, such as the EU education project "ERASMUS" (伊拉斯谟协议) plan through the German academic exchange center (DAAD) etc. In 2005 the German academic exchange center attracts 12,000 European students to study in German universities funded by the Erasmus program to study in Germany.

In order to attract foreign top scholars and researchers to work in German universities, research institutions in Federal Ministry of Education set up a total subsidy of 10 million euros by Humboldt foundation (洪堡基金). In addition Alexander von Humboldt Foundation in Federal Ministry of Education supports the establishment of German teacher flow to obtain more academic information from other universities and research institutions. In 2004/2005 year about 2,600 German scholars and teachers are funded by Erasmus program to exchange academic visits.

(5) Teacher Education System Reform

It can be seen that German teacher education forms a structured training system. In 2005 the education ministers in Bergen Conference (卑尔根会议) requires to strengthen teachers' interdisciplinary education and the cultivation of vocational ability in order to strengthen the guidance and assessment on teachers education.

As a result German universities pay more attention to the construction of teachers' interdisciplinary education, attempting scientific methods of teaching and cultivation of comprehensive quality in teachers' education. Promoting life-long education and research is formulated with the strategy of "German Lifelong Education". The strategy aims to promote and support all teachers in the field of their study, which will broaden the innovation of teaching, learning and culture input. In addition more flexible teaching organization, part-time education and remote education are legally recognized and mixed with teachers' requirements.

1.2.4 Teacher Education in Sweden

Twenty nine national ministers of the ministry of education in Europe, including members of the European Union, negotiated to build European higher education area and improve the common European higher education system on June 1999. The meeting was successful and the ministers signed "Bologna Declaration".

The focus of the Bologna Declaration is to build understanding and international education system when committed to build a two-phase model based on higher education system then establish credit system (European credit transfer system). To promote teachers and students' academic flow Swedish universities overcome the barriers to mobility and guarantee the quality of European higher education. Gradually Swedish universities are targeted to promote the English teachers'education within the scope of cooperation.

Bologna Process is a long-term plan and the goal is to set up a common European higher education system in that the meeting on behalf of the proposed process should keep continuous attention and support in the future since the council of ministers, supervision and evaluation in Bologna Process will accelerate teachers' education in Sweden.

Sweden is one of the participating countries in Bologna Process with the goal of implementing integration of European higher education to improve the competitive ability of teachers' education. European and American students start to flow in the beginning of Swedish higher education reform for Swedish higher education information technology has created new opportunities and new ways of university teaching. Swedish universities perform a lifelong education mode so the new network learning mode adapts to university teaching as soon as possible after a number of European countries exchange students with Swedish universities. Swedish education department's attitude is popular with the development of international network learning and finally Swedish universities develop worldwide network learning system. It can be seen that the globalization of Swedish higher education in Bologna Process relies on the development of online education and teacher education.

(1) Online Virtual University

In 2001 the Swedish government submitted a bill to Congress, asking Congress to establish a national virtual university funding. After the parliamentary debate the bill was adopted to allocate $20 million annual funding. So far the Swedish government sponsors online virtual university funding by more than 200 million US dollars.

In order to fulfill the Bologna agreement as soon as possible to promote international education, Swedish Virtual University officially open online registration for the first batch of 2,350 students in the Bologna Process who have become the first lucky ones. There are 39 accredited universities in Sweden, among which 30 virtual universities appeared in Sweden and distributed throughout the country from the densely populated southern region to the north of Sweden. With the impact of ubiquitous virtual university students do not go to school class instead self-learning through the network is necessary to submit online homework.

There is a problem of language use since Swedish is not the official language instruction. English has become a virtual alternative to Swedish university teaching language. It is based on its international considerations. Swedish government's goal is to build a network across the EU Virtual University, which uses English as their medium of instruction. Due to the popularity of the Internet online virtual university is popular with teachers' education in Sweden. Until 2010 the Christmas after the new school year began, the number of students in Swedish virtual university reached 10 million people, which is a great thing to a small country. The reason why Swedish favors virtual university reflects their quiet life at home to receive university education and the number of elderly people in Sweden will also accept the network self-learning in their lifelong learning concept.

Since 2002 Swedish government has set up a network university authority the government continues to strengthen the application and popularization of computer knowledge. Every university teacher receives a free computer network training which effectively promotes the development of virtual university. In the end of June 2009 the country has more than eight million Internet users while the Internet penetration rate is as high as 95%.

For the instance of the famous University of Uppsala many adult students in the university are registered as virtual university students and usually they need to regularly attend seminars organized by universities.

(2) Autonomous Learning and Credit system

With the accelerated process of development in Bologna Process online resources are enjoyed in EU and America. These data are also related with Sweden in some advanced subject knowledge or information through the network access. The online learning speeds up the autonomous learning progress with development of Swedish universities.

Educational technology reflects teaching modernization. By the end of 2009 the cable installation means that the majority of the members of the family can rely on satellite cable television network in autonomous learning. Network courses gradually rely on the satellite cable television as English generally becomes Swedish official language and the content of knowledge so that Swedish teachers'education is easily implemented via English channels of satellite cable television. Swedish National Internet popularity almost reached every family in 2009.

Swedish university students progress with strong learning motivation. The autonomous learning is not completely independent learning, but participating in some university academic activities on a regular basis. Recent studies show that in the process of Swedish network learning teachers' guidance activities continue to increase while registered students are demanded to attend some professional lectures. The web-based autonomous learning and teachers' teaching is combined through face to face communication with the assessment organization named Teaching Quality Committee of twelve members. The network learning scale of Swedish university students increases throughout EU after 2010 implementation.

Flexible credit system in Swedish network teaching reflects the flexibility and diversity of teachers'classroom teaching as a result of the Bologna process in EU countries to achieve the mutual recognition of credits. All countries in the EU will recognize Swedish credits each other. In addition independent online learning credits can also be converted into American university credits effectively in promoting the internationalization process of online course. Development of Swedish network courses are accompanied by English teachers'education and training.

(3) Rapid Development of Individual Learning Accounts

Since January 2002 the Swedish government has started the individual learning account program. Sweden individual learning account system has been basically established through the virtual university funding in the network learning. The establishment of individual learning accounts is funded by the Swedish University Network Foundation because financial problems usually lead to students'dropping out in learning process.

Individual learning accounts apply to every online learner and every university online learner will benefit from their own personal account withdrawals for network learning, but enough money in individual learning account will be saved for at least one year. Swedish students will extract money for their own network and independent learning universities regularly organize seminars and academic activities at the same time.

Due to government regulations for special purposes of individual learning accounts Swedish teachers will find effective ways to achieve lifelong learning with the development of the Bologna Process. The individual learning account management assumes socialization. Moreover teachers and students are encouraged to exchange academic ideas for specific learning objectives in order to effectively monitor online teaching efficiency. In general Swedish government demands online teaching universities and educational institutions to have complete course plans, learning programs and specific content.

1.2.5 Teacher Education in Finland

Finland implemented university education system since1995. Finnish teacher education reform consists of two stages. The first phase includes teacher master education within two years; the second phase belongs to PhD studies. Teachers' education system in Finland is transitional in reality so as to prepare for further adjustment in Bologna Process. Master degree is the basic university teacher degree. To cope with Bologna Declaration for higher education in Finland university teachers' education corresponds to adjustment and reform for teachers' scientific research and development.

(1) Degree Structure Reform

In 2005 Bologna Declaration proposed to establish a three-degree system in European context, that is, three years of undergraduate education, two years of postgraduate education and three years of PhD education. The first and second degree stage should have different requirements and forms in order to accommodate the individual, academic and labor market needs.

In 2006 the new "Finnish University Degree Law" is promulgated in addition to the three-tier degree system. Master degree is mandatory to university teachers'conditions. The new degree structure also applies to English teachers based on career-oriented professional degree. On August 2006 the second stage of multidisciplinary teaching ability came into effect. Back in the mid-1990s Finland put forward bilingual language teaching to supplement statutory obligation.

(2) Establishment of Credit Transfer and Accumulation System

On August 2005 the European Credit Transfer System (ECTS) replaced the original Finnish national credit system. The basic calculation of ECTS is 180 ~ 240 credits in the first stage and 90 ~ 120 credits for the second stage. In the old credit system one credit needs about 40 hours of study (including lectures and other forms of courses, exercises, seminars and self-study at home or in the library).

In the new system the average of 1,600 hours in a year of work equals to 60 ECTS credits and students'learning burden will be reduced accordingly. The new credit system is also applicable to polytechnics. European Credit Transfer System on the basis of undergraduate and graduate education is convertible and comparable degree system, thereby promoting the most widespread student mobility, and actively promoting teacher education in Finland to adjust to ECTS.

(3) Establishing a Scientific Quality Assurance System

Bergen conference emphasizes on education quality assurance and accreditation, which accelerates international competitions among Finnish universities. The results show that Finland is the best in quality assurance of higher education. Finnish Higher Education Evaluation Council Regulation details responsibilities of Finnish Higher Education Evaluation Council (FINHEEC, 芬兰高等教育董事会) in international cooperation, teacher education and scientific research to provide assessment and criteria for university innovation.

1 – 5 **Bergen Conference**

1 – 6 **Bologna Process in Finland**

FINHEEC members are appointed by the Ministry of Education, which consists of two branches. Commission (Polytechnic and Vocational Courses Certification Commission for Certification Board) have student and teacher representatives in accordance with the principles of diversification and transparency in FINHEEC during the different stages of quality assessment. Teacher and student representatives will participate in planning and decision-making process. During the evaluation process views of the majority of students and teachers are proposed by way of questionnaires and interviews and seminars are available to teachers'teaching quality. Finland is one of the few countries signatory to the students as the external evaluation team members.

Higher Education in the five Nordic countries has always had a tradition of cooperation to expand the scope of cooperation in the field of higher education quality assessment. Finland is a member of the Nordic higher education quality assurance of the network, which provides a platform for discussion and exchange in teachers' assessment. In addition Finland is one of the European Higher Education Quality Assurance Association (ENQA).

University Law (Amendment Act) shows that all Finnish universities must evaluate their teacher education and research to publish the results of teacher assessment. In University of Helsinki the evaluation on teacher research and education is held every year at the University. On the internal assessment Helsinki University has developed its own set of teacher educational guarantee system and established Finnish Teacher Education Evaluation Council at the end of 2007. The policy of Finnish Ministry of Education will be subject to inspection on teacher education because the development and acceptance of quality assurance inspection system will have become an important part of the realization of European Higher Education Area by 2010.

(4) Promoting Mobility and International Curriculum Development

Finland has implemented internationalization degree system reform since 1999. Finnish government greatly promotes Finnish education with the internationalization of education standards as the only strategic policy development in Finland.

In 2001 the committee appointed by the Finnish Ministry of Education for Higher Education drafted the "Finnish International Development Strategy Report". Finnish university will compete for the best students and teachers in universities. By 2010 Finland has 10,000 to 15,000 foreign exchange students. The Commission made a number of development measures: Finland degree structures and credit systems toward more international comparability of the direction of reform while developing additional foreign language courses is to ensure the quality of teaching and focus on comparative advantage in Finnish academic skills and knowledge.

"Finnish university degree Law" and "University Law" (Amendment Act) aims to encourage the University to participate in international cooperation and development of joint degree programs. In 2004 the Finnish Ministry of Education issued a joint International Teaching Development Proposal.

CBU, a Russian cross-border University in Finland is an example of the development of teachers' education with the purpose to establish a joint master's degree program to improve and deepen cooperation in education at the University between Finland and Russia. The co-financed is provided by an implementation project in Finland. In addition the EU's Erasmus program also provides many English courses in Finland.

In addition to EU's plan Finland is also involved in a number of Nordic cooperation programs in teacher education to cooperate with other countries of the world. In spring of 2007 the European Network of Information Center (ENIC) and the National Academic Recognition Information Center (NARIC) organized a seminar in China and India where Finnish teacher education experience is presented. Now Finnish universities will compete with other European universities to recruit international joint degree programs and other programs for students. Hence teacher education and training become urgent in Finland.

(5) Strengthening Scientific Cooperation and Exchange

In Berlin meeting it stressed the importance of teachers' scientific research, training and interdisciplinary education in improving the quality and competitive importance.

Bologna Process in Finland aims to encourage cross-border cooperation in teachers'scientific research and training. International cooperation with teachers'scientific research is a tradition in Finland for Finland is not only abundant in research funds and flexible funding mechanism, but also allows researchers and university teachers to do research abroad or become visiting scholars.

In 2005 Finland's national research funding accounted for 3.5% of GDP. Academy of Finland establishes a cooperative agreement with 26 countries until 2013. Under these agreements Academy grants 1.7 million euros to support the international mobility of teachers and researchers in the long term or short term visit or study. In addition the Centre for International Mobility (CIMO, 芬兰教育部国际交流中心) offers short-term visiting scholar and ELT training abroad.

1.2.5 Teacher Education in Spain

(1) Social Needs-oriented Training Objectives

To guarantee the quality of higher education in Spain, the sub-project "Tuning Educational Structures in Europe" (欧洲高等教育结构调整计划) as European higher education reform plan in Bologna Process is put into effect through economic changes. Social needs and all comprehensive researches involve nine disciplines (mathematics, geology, history, European studies, nursing, chemistry, physics, business management). The overall professional competence in universities requires curriculum reform programs and teacher education reform in order to reach a consensus in that curriculum development, quality improvement and teacher education in Spanish colleges and universities will adjust them to European higher education reform.

The strategic plan presided by University of Barcelona (UB) over the comprehensive standards of excellent teachers achieves its objective and target for the criteria to judge the higher education quality in Spain.

Selecting and determining the training objectives of professional teachers in Spanish universities have been extensive investigation and consultation in consideration of interests of teachers and stakeholders of employers and community on the basis of expectation on academic community or professional competence (general and professional capacity) in response of curriculum design and teacher education.

Spain formulates teacher education training objectives with considering the mutual recognition of academic system, European free movement of labor force policy, teacher quality structure and other factors, which aims to train teachers with formal education to reach the target of relevant social admission.

(2) Quality Standards of Competency-based Teacher Education

Higher Education Curriculum System in Spain follows the new "European Educational Restructuring Plan" (欧洲高等教育再调整计划) to target teacher ability, which will focus on teachers' development and comprehensive account of the expected teaching outcomes in order to meet professional quality requirements. On teachers' professional requirements it includes training of professional knowledge and skills to master basic skills and specific education involving a wide range of evaluation.

Teacher education in Spain involves understanding objectives, course content and assessment criteria to promote and facilitate teachers' learning in globalization. Teachers are required with diverse backgrounds to design and specify the teaching process and cooperation inside and outside universities. Such factors as individuality, intellectual and moral development will be considered. Understanding the characteristics of language development will be able to be identified to ensure teachers' normal development. Of course ELT becomes a developing strategy in Spanish universities. To understand and assess teacher education has become an organizational strategy and professional skills.

As is seen above Spanish teachers education involves teachers' physical and mental development, so it is essentially based on the development of professional development and teacher quality with target-related education and teaching ability to achieve the expected development goals.

Teacher education is certainly reasonable and unquestionable superiority in Spanish Higher Education Training Objectives. The principle reflects evident traces that require not only the ability to develop the kind of behavior, and also implicitly the areas of life in which teachers can use this behavior or content.

(3) Curriculum Integration

Strictly speaking curriculum integration is common in combination of curriculum type made by a variety of courses. Judging from course traces it is of an integrated curriculum in the form of a single curriculum framework which accommodates a wide knowledge of curriculum contents and teaching methods, such as teaching and learning plan, social science teaching, language teaching etc.

From the philosophy point of view, it is embodied in the curriculum with teachers'developing orientation and contents of subject knowledge. According to the actual situation of teacher education as well as specific teaching situation it demands for knowledge and skills of teachers, who set up different genres, different types of activities and methods of teaching skills. Such cognitive developing theory is reflected in Spanish teacher education.

(4) Balanced and Reasonable Course Structure

Course structure refers to different teaching schedule in different types of courses to form a type of organizational system. It is perceived that teaching experiences meets three basic criteria: continuity, innovation and integration—they are the basic guidelines to construct a framework for the organization of an effective teaching experience.

Under Bologna Process European Credit Accumulation and Transfer System (ECTS) have become common basis for course structure design and teacher education in Spain. Course structure design has also introduced some teacher education modules in Spanish universities.

From the vertical structure the curriculum system with sequential continuity, in general, is better integrated in Spain. Spanish universities set up communicative competence development programs in teacher education and education programs. English language teaching pedagogy is integrated into curriculum design and ELT is growing important in teacher education, which reflects the continuity of the courses in teacher education. Course curriculum system requires teachers' creation in a sequential curriculum.

Overall the course curriculum design covers the field of psychology, education, sociology, ELT and other theoretical basis. Spanish teachers come to realize that learning contexts of higher education is a part of necessary knowledge and skills. To some extent highlighting the integrated curriculum has become a necessary skill to Spanish teacher education.

1.3 Enlightenments of Teacher Education in Europe and America

The current teacher education policy in the EU has contained richer content, such as building a common teacher standard, improving the quality of teacher education, promoting teachers' in-service professional development and improving the construction mechanism of teacher team etc. With committed demands of European integration in EU more English teachers come to realize the integration urgency of teacher education, construction of teacher education index system and standards for teacher ability. So there are two aspects of approaches for English Language Teaching. The first aspect is from teachers' self-development and self-learning in their career change. And the second part is the approaches to teachers' development and learning.

First internationalization has become the driving force of the reform and development in higher education. And influenced by Bologna process both internationalization of higher education and university cooperation should provide a good opportunity to become the propeller of university teacher education reform. Hence it must be integrated into the international environment of higher education, conforming to the international trend of development, actively participating in international cooperation and international competition, deepening the internationalization of higher education reform and development as a powerful external driving force.

Second the internationalization of structural elements and information elements becomes the core content of higher education reform. Internationalization of higher education refers to the higher education around the world through mutual exchanges, which aims to learn from each other. Interaction, mutual competition and melting as a whole activity process and developing trend, are mainly reflected in information elements and structural elements. The influence of the economic globalization of higher education, profoundly manifests talent training quality, knowledge, ability structure and teaching methods etc. Cultivating talents in higher education must adapt to economic globalization situation, the need for talent quality, the growing international economic exchange and national competition. Hence we must constantly update education idea, reform teacher training target, course system, teaching contents and teaching methods etc. At the same time the internationalization of information elements must be supported by the internationalization of structural elements, teaching management structure such as credit system, evaluation system, internationalization of the academic degree system etc. From European higher education reform in the Bologna Process it can be seen that information elements and internationalization structure have become the core content of higher education reform. Information elements and international community will drive and promote the internationalization of university teacher education. For domestic colleges and universities, attaching importance to international cooperation and exchange, emphasizing on structural elements (e. g. teacher education, degree system, credit system, evaluation system, teaching organization, teaching management structure etc.) and information elements (e. g. teacher training target, specialty setting, curriculum system, teaching contents, teaching methods etc.) will be of vitality in the international community.

External quality evaluation system in structural elements has become an important means to improve the international competitiveness of higher education. For a long time teaching and research areas in European and American universities have enjoyed a high degree of autonomy, thereby higher education has a long tradition of academic freedom and teaching quality assurance is based on self-discipline. On entering the 21st century more and more international competition focuses on talents competition, which demands change of external quality evaluation system in universities. At present the major teaching evaluation in China is still the government-leading when government approval is given priority. Hence construction of effective professional certification and teacher evaluation mechanism is indispensible.

Third it is necessary to deepen the dialogue mechanism of teacher education policy. In EU and its member states it is necessary to recognize teacher education as development of the whole education career, which even has the major effect on regional development. The European Union adopts the open method in coordination through peer learning activities to strengthen dialogue and cooperation in the EU and its member states to build dialogue mechanism of teacher education policy. The open method of coordination as a policy of cooperation and dialogue mechanism among the member states is not just limited to teacher education policy but through the cooperation mechanism. Since 2005 the teacher education policy in peer learning activity has covered the theme of teacher education policy, pre-service teacher education, classroom practice training policy, in-service professional development of teachers and trainers etc. Although European commission is not forcing different countries to agree on a consistent teacher education policy, each member in a certain extent reaches a consensus on teacher education policy to improve mutual understanding. The consensus will endow different countries to provide a variety of policy choice in objective effect on European Union education policy and education reform.

Fourth teacher education, vocational education and in-service professional development are advantageous to teachers' career development. Therefore EU begins to advocate the integration of teacher education and release the corresponding policy decision in order to implement this idea. As the Council Resolution on the professional development points out that university teachers' professional development covers pre-service teacher education, vocational education and in-service professional development in a coherent process. Among them the pre-service teacher education includes both theoretical study and teaching practice to ensure the high quality of pre-service teachers training. University entry education requires a bridging pre-service education and in-service professional development. Strengthening the professional education can help new teachers to adapt to the new working environment as soon as possible and reduce teachers' pressure. The purpose of in-service professional development activities is to help teachers to update the knowledge, skills and ideas and make it adaptable to the pace of society. European Union in separate resolution files also stresses that European cooperation in pre-service teacher education, professional education and in-service professional development will be an important stage of cohesion in order to realize the integration of teacher education. Education is the integration of teacher education and professional education. To maximum extent EU is increasing in-service teacher education, vocational education and in-service professional development in the areas of policy support and influence to build communication platform and fulfill peer learning activities in that teachers' self-evaluation will determine the demand of teachers' professional development, which provides adequate developing opportunities for ELT teachers.

Fifth it is beneficial to construct the index system of teacher education. Teacher education quality monitoring and evaluation has become a bottleneck restricting the development of teacher education. Building the index system of teacher education comes from the concrete future objectives of education systems. Specifically this target is focused on quality and efficiency of education training system in implementation of extensive education training system. Among them the first major category is targeted at training of ELT teachers. For English teachers providing the high quality of pre-service education and in-service development opportunities appeal to ensure teachers' professional standard. They may be stimulated to participate in continuing professional development. In addition modern information communication technology (ICT) will be integrated into English teachers' education in order to promote teachers' development system as well as teachers' working environment. Corpus teaching training is essential to help improve the quality of English teacher education and professional development with the implementation of modern English teaching pedagogy.

Sixth teachers' education programs must keep up with high quality to meet demand of professional teachers in universities. Teachers have to be faced with high academic standard and practical teaching experience to enhance teacher education quality. Therefore universities need to focus on teachers' education career, in-depth research and professional development of their selection and qualification that are related to research project. In order to stimulate relevant teacher education qualification and ability team research is a good way to promote teacher education, which mainly includes problem definition, types, roles, responsibilities, qualification and ability in teacher education. Definitely team research and peer teaching activities will help English teachers achieve their goals.

In a word the Bologna Process proposed by EU and its member states implements the construction of teachers education in European professional development and assessment framework together with teacher qualification and standard to match normalization and standardization of European level, thus providing reference standard and policy support for other countries which will regulate university teacher education qualifications effectively. Besides the current teacher education policy in EU and America contains rich content and reflects a series of development trend of teacher education. These policy contents, policy directions and development trends definitely influence English teachers education in the world. Simutaneously EU provides all kinds of education to implement and build the diversification path, effectively ensuring the implementation of teachers' education, which provides the reference standard to teachers' qualification. In another word a teacher education mechanism is built with a variety of professional developing platform.

Bibliography

[1] European Commission. Common European Principles for Teachers Competences and Qualifications [Z]. 2005.

[2] Conclusions of the Council and of the Representatives of the Governments of the Member States Meeting within the Council of 15 November 2007 on Improving the Quality of Teacher education [J]. Official Journal of the European Union, 2007 - 12 - 12: C300/6 - C300/9.

[3] Council Conclusion of 26 November 2009 on the Professional Development of Teachers and School Leaders [J]. Official Journal of the European Union, 2009 - 12 - 12: C302/8.

[4] European Commission. Commission Staff Working Document Supporting the Teaching Professions for Better Learning outcomes [R]. Strasbourg, 2012: 28.

[5] Council of the European Union. Council Conclusions on the Professional Development of Teachers and School Leaders [Z]. Brussels, 2009 - 12 - 06.

[6] Conclusions of the Council and of the Representatives of the Governments of the Member States Meeting within the Council of 21 November 2008 on Preparing Young People for the 21st Century: an Agenda for European Coopera-

tion on Schools [J]. Official Journal of the European Union, 2008 - 12 - 13: C319/20.

[7] 徐立新:《博洛尼亚进程下欧盟教师教育的探索与创新》,《比较教育研究》2011 年第 7 期。

注　　解

1. 博洛尼亚进程(Bologna Process):1999 年欧洲 29 个国家在意大利博洛尼亚提出了欧洲高等教育改革计划,该计划的目标是整合欧盟的高教资源,打通教育体制。"博洛尼亚进程"的发起者和参与国家希望,到 2010 年欧洲"博洛尼亚进程"签约国中任何一个国家大学毕业生的毕业证书和成绩,都将获得其他签约国家的承认,大学毕业生可以毫无障碍地在其他欧洲国家申请学习硕士阶段的课程或者寻找就业机会,实现欧洲高教和科技一体化,建成欧洲高等教育区,为欧洲一体化进程作出贡献。

2. 英语教育(ELT, English Language Teaching):主要培养具有扎实的英语语言基础知识和语言基本技能、较熟练的英语语言运用能力和具有先进的教育理念,熟悉教育基本规律,能够使用现代化教学手段和方法的英语教师。

3. 国际教育协会(Association of International Education):是获得国际认可的专门从事职业培训认证、信息咨询、行业期刊编撰的国际性教育组织。协会可在海外和香港两地注册,致力于通过教育推动社会的发展,通过专业的执业知识体系和系统的认证标准为各国培养财务、金融、法律、管理、营销、市场等方面的行业高端人才,并为这些人才提供终身的教育机会。协会下设多个专业协会,遍布全球,分亚太、欧洲、美洲、非洲、中东分部,会员由各行各业的精英组成。

4. 欧洲学分制(ETCS):欧洲学分积累与转换系统,由课程单元、学习负荷量、学业水平和高等教育机构的"标签"等重要因素构成。欧洲学分制最突出的成就是促进了欧盟国家的学生流动,进而成为推动欧洲高等教育一体化进程的重要工具。该系统属于欧共体管理计划,也就是现在的欧盟教育领域的苏格拉底 - 伊拉斯谟(SOCRATES - ERASMUS)计划。

Chapter Two ELT and Teacher Education

English language teaching (ELT) has been a widely used term after Bologna Process. From the perspectives of information theory, the process of education is the process of information spreading. It is reinforced by the interaction of education resource and education target. English language teachers play an important role in the teaching activities of European and American universities since Bologna Process. Teachers' comprehensive qualities and language levels are considered sufficient guarantee of university teaching quality. At present ELT is met with great challenge of how to create situations for the students morally, intelligently and academically, which puts forward demand for English teachers' education.

2.1 Professional Education of English Teachers

Change is a constant assurance in contemporary society after Bologna Process. The mandate of schools and universities, of course, is to educate people in order to help them meet the challenges that tomorrow will bring because of these changes. It is literally impossible today for a teacher to take on teaching job and remain in it for long time with his or her teaching skills unchanged. There are some conditions that teachers are usually accustomed to old teaching contents and methods which are out of date since they are lazy to innovate and create.

Since Bologna Process in the end of 1990s, experts and researchers have been studying about English Teacher education and development. Significant advances have been made in understanding, explaining and exploring the concept of Teacher Development and its relationship with many other aspects in education. The questions put forward such motives as what Teacher Development is or how Teacher Development initiates English language teaching so as to make us devote more attention to understanding the importance and significance of the teachers' teaching and self-refinement.

2 - 1 **Teacher Training**

2 - 2 **English—A Language to You**

The term Teacher Development comes into vogue more than ten years ago. Many educational researchers have made studies on how English teachers become more efficient and productive in teaching. In some ways, linking teacher development to successful implementation of innovation is straightforward. Joyce and Showers (2008) have shown that Teacher Development is central to instructional changes of teaching models. English teachers should be equipped with theory-demonstration and practice-feedback that appeared in their practical teaching. Carr and Kemmis (1983) consider further statements that teacher development can be judged, assessed and evaluated through students' outcome and promotion in personality, cognitive styles, learning strategies and motivation. Stallings (2009) shows in specific points of view that the relationship between teacher development and change in teaching practice is summarized as following:

(1) They become aware of a need for improvement through their analysis of their own observation-profile.

(2) They make a written commitment to try new ideas in their classroom the next day.

(3) They modify the workshop ideas to work in their classroom and school.

(4) They try the ideas and evaluate the effect.

(5) They observe in each other's classrooms and analyze their own data.

(6) They report their success or failure to their group.

(7) They discuss problems and solutions regarding individual students and/or teaching subject matter.

(8) They need a wide variety of approaches: modeling, simulations, observations, reviewing videotapes, presenting at professional meetings.

(9) They learn in their own continuity to set new goals for professional growth.

(Stallings 2009: 3 -4)

Fullan and Hargreaves (1992) point out that teacher education and development must actively listen to teacher's voice and establish opportunities for English teachers to confront with the assumptions and beliefs underlying their practices; secondly it will avoid faddism and blanket implementation of favored new instructional strategies and create a community of teachers who discuss and develop their purposes together over time.

Development involves teachers' growth for their own aspects of how to do something new in curriculum materials, instructional practices and behaviors. The implementation of these aspects provides teachers with more chances to promote tendencies towards new skills and practices.

With studies on teacher education and development going deeper and with the school administrators and teachers accepting the concept and applying it in ELT, people come to recognize some unsettled issues that arise in operation. Those problems with which we might be faced are as follows:

(1) Lack of sustained central office support and follow-through;

(2) Trying to do too much with too little support;

(3) Underfeeding the project, or trying to do too much with too little support;

(4) Lack of technical assistance and other forms of intensive teacher development;

(5) Lack of awareness of the limitations of teachers and school administers' knowledge about how to implement the project;

(6) Failure to address the incompatibility between project requirements and existing organizational policies and structures;

(7) Failure to understand and take into account site-specific differences among universities.

It is believed that the above points of view will be barriers for successful operations in English language teachers' professional development. How to initiate a wider context of implementation in curriculums, practices and behaviors still make us consider it comprehensively. Many theories and researches do not tell us much to know about the relationship between teacher development and individual teacher's purpose, the teacher as a person and his working conditions. Fullan and Hargreaves (1991) list the paradigms of other elements for English teacher education and development and help us to see some development strategies:

(1) English teachers' developing purpose;

(2) Teacher development as a person;

(3) The real context in which English teachers work;

(4) Teaching culture: the working relationship that teachers have with their colleagues inside and outside universities.

English language teaching is a very subtle and complicated activity. There are many things that teachers desire for. They hope to achieve through their teaching. But there are also things that teacher devalue. These things might make teaching worse. Generally teachers are divided into good or bad, responsible or irresponsible in their university teaching. Hence English teacher as a person has been neglected in their development. Many elements such as age, personality, cognitive styles, stage of career and life experiences also make up a complete person. Once these aspects used for teacher development are ignored, problems will arise. For example, we mighty always pay more attention to the experienced teachers who have been working for years in universities.

On the other hand we pay no attention to novice teachers because they just graduate from college and have no teaching experiences and achievements. Fewer chances are given to them for the promotion of their teaching. Next is about the contexts in which teachers work. The administrators in universities and government conduct language curriculum construction and design to English Teachers. Teachers are offered fewer opportunities to participate in curriculum innovations. Some curriculum designs are separated from the practical teaching, taking little account of the social contexts in which learning and teaching take place. The culture of teaching also works effectively for teacher education and development. University cultures should provide teachers with collaborative work in which ELT and Teacher Development are motivated and encouraged.

The research of teacher development indeed creates a new field for the professional development of teacher education. It is only in more than ten years that teacher development as a concept comes to be recognized and accepted by experts and practitioners. Although some assumptions are abstract and superficial, reforms in ELT continue to achieve more in teacher education and development of European and American universities.

2 - 3 **ELT in University of Barcelona (UB)**

2 - 4 **ELT in UCLA**

（注：笔者在西班牙巴塞罗那大学和美国洛杉矶加利福尼亚大学研究欧美教师教育）

Today the tasks and responsibilities of English teachers are more complex and demanding than in the past. They have to respond to the wishes of students' parent regarding educational outcomes, the social need for wider access to education, and pressures for more democratic participation in universities. Since societies throughout the world are constantly changing and developing, English teachers are expected to make changes based on their professional experience. Especially at the beginning of the new century, English teachers act as main characters in the educational movement. Changes, reforms and improvements influence primarily upon English teachers. They are professional group who has to implement the formulations and specifications laid down by the educational policy makers. As a result teachers' education and training are the most important and significant experiences in their life-long teaching career. What McNiff said has impressed us deeply:

I believe that those who want to learn do the best teaching. I consider how I have transformed my own life through critically reflecting on what I am doing in all aspects of life. I recognize myself as a changing individual in a changing world. 1 change my thought as my thought changes me. I am open-minded to life, and delighted in my own learning. I feel crucially that this is what teaching is about: the ability of an open-minded individual to bring her learners to the point where they, too, may be open to their own process of self-development. I feel this may be done by the effort of teachers to establish the frameworks of care in which learners may develop their own understanding of their own experiences. I think teachers who have the key to their own process of self-improvement by acknowledging that, too, are travelers, and still have far to go.

(McNiff 1993: 10)

Teaching as learning for promoting teachers' growth should be in three dimensions including the development of professional expertise, psychological development and teaching situation. The process of teaching is the process of learning. Leithwood briefs six stages about the procedures of English teachers' ongoing learning in professional expertise:

(1) Developing survival skills;

(2) Becoming competent in the basic skills of instruction;

(3) Expanding one's instructional flexibility;

(4) Acquiring instructional expertise;

(5) Contributing to the growth of colleagues' instructional expertise;

(6) Participating in a broad array of educational decisions at all levels.

(Leithwood 1992: 89)

Stage 1 – 4 is concerned with English teachers' classroom responsibilities. In these stages, language teachers must possess the adequate knowledge about professions and techniques including phonology, lexicology, pragmatics, semantics and language competence. They enhance their competence of instructional organizations and applications by knowing well about pedagogy, psychology and methodology. Stage 5 – 6 addresses clearly how the mature and experienced teachers would act when they have higher levels of expertise in classroom performance and are able to exercise leadership and understand among decisions at many different levels in the educational system. Here the word "leadership" should be understood broadly. It does not only mean English teachers must be principals or administrators in education system. In addition it means that they lead in academics, professions and researches. They can be called models in teaching and set good examples for other teachers.

The second dimension is about the psychological development. The process of teaching is the process of learning, in another word, the process of psychological development. At the beginning of their teaching performance, they are self-protective and dependent. The classroom performance is teacher-directed. At the second stage, they might like peers and find identity from their colleagues. Nevertheless they hold distrustful views of other people. With their acquiring instructional expertise and contributing to further growth of colleagues' instructional expertise, English teachers become more self-conscious and autonomous in their own teaching and learning. They are integrated in teaching performance, developing a student-centered model.

Learning in professional expertise and psychology is reciprocal and supportive. Professional expertise can help the development of English teacher thinking and teacher thinking can motivate teachers' professional development and instructional skills. In a traditional view the acting of teaching involves passing on the skills and concepts to learners. The classroom is teacher-oriented. In educational innovation, a teacher should work as a monitor, consultant and helper. The students are self-directed in learning under the teachers' guidance. With development of teachers'self-awareness and autonomy, they will have teacher-centered models and more chances in shifting their beliefs to student-centered modes in that education aims to develop the individual rationality and to teach people how to think.

Not only professional expertise and psychological development will help teachers' teaching as learning, but also teaching situations can initiate and broaden the on-going learning in professional development. Classrooms, however, are complex places where activities occur and overlap. English Teachers can learn a lot from classroom observation. Wajuryb (1999) regards that classroom observation seeks to provide stimulus and ideas for ways of exploring one's own teaching by observing other teachers. It takes a skilled and trained eye to perceive, understand and benefit from observing the proceedings of learning and teaching. Hence English teachers can learn from the classroom observation:

—to discover the focus and clarity;

—to collect classroom-based data about teaching;

—to raise self-awareness and reflect on the classroom;

—to make classroom more informed and systematic by getting more chances of decision-making;

—to understand effectively the relationship between theory and practice;

—to foster mutual respect and help through collaborative work in classroom observation;

The process of English teachers' learning in classroom observation is an active one, not a passive one. As Wajuryb describes:

In this view of learning, the teacher does not learn solely by acquiring new information or knowledge about teaching (such as new procedures or techniques), but through thinking about new ideas into her or his thinking, and reappearing in old assumptions in the light of new information. New information is therefore absorbed in a way that is creative, dynamic and personal and that will mean something different to each person receiving the information.

(Wajuryb 1999: 10)

However in practical teaching it is accepted by some English teachers. Their concept of teaching as learning is not recognized to develop their professional skills and instructions. They tend not to pursue the ego, moral expertise in the basic concept development, which motivate people respectively to integrate experiences, enjoy collaboration with teachers. Furthermore when some teachers reach a professional plateau, they seem to stop striving for promotion and simply enjoy teaching.

It should be remembered that teaching as learning is a life-long project for English teacher development. The process of a teacher's teaching is the process of his learning, in which he gives free rein to his intellectual curiosity and uses his deepened insights to move forward.

2.2 Teaching as Researching and Learning

Language teachers cannot only learn from classroom, but also do research for teacher development. Classroom is the setting for English teachers to give knowledge to students in that teachers have further studies about it. Connecting theory with practice is the practical way for both sides to achieve effective teaching and learning results. As Widdowson clarifies:

In my view, the value of research is that it can help English teachers to define more clearly the Problems that they themselves must solve. What it can do is to stimulate interest and encourage teachers to think about the implications of their practices. It can also provide them with a conceptual context within which to work, in the form of hypotheses to test out in the conditions of their particular classrooms. In short theory can help practitioners to adopt a theoretical orientation to their task, whereby they seek to refer the particular techniques they use to more general principles, and, reciprocally, test out the validity of such principles against the observed actualities of classroom practice.

(Widdowson 2001: 25 – 26)

English teachers, then, can participate in a research activity whereby experimental techniques of instruction, are designed to correspond with principles of pedagogy. Through experimental research and practical application, the validity of principles and the utility of techniques are mutually adjusted to each other.

Of course language teachers have extra commitments. They cannot just only act as researchers and use students as experimental subjects and observe how they learn under different kinds of conditions to satisfy their theoretical and intellectual curiosity. English teachers' responsibilities are to discover how teaching techniques and learning strategies work effectively in classroom. Widdowson (2001) refers that English teachers become intervening variables in their own experiments in effect. Their research has to be applied in the very process of inquiry: it has to be directly accountable in terms of practical pay-off.

If so we can perceive classroom as the context for two related kinds of activity. On the one hand, techniques are applied to benefit students for their practical effectiveness in the promotion of learning. This might be called the instructional activity, with the teachers applying the techniques. On the other hand, the techniques are related to principles with a view inquiring into the relationship between the two sides. Here the techniques help English teachers to understand their teaching methods and skills used in the classroom. This might be called the experimental activity. In classroom English teachers act as observers to operate the techniques and principles needed for teaching. The experimental activity and instructional activity are reciprocally enhanced. The two sides act together to inform and reinforce each other.

The practice of language teaching for English teachers' research work rests on a readiness on the part of practitioners to pursue their own inquires in the very process of classroom teaching. Regarding to classroom teaching Stenhouse (1975) gives his statement:

The uniqueness of each classroom setting implies that any proposal-even at university level needs to be tested, verified, and adapted by each teacher in his own classroom. The ideal is that the curricular specification should feed a teacher's personal research and development programs through which he is increasing his understanding of his own work and hence better his teaching.

(Stenhouse1975: 43)

In 1980s the "teacher as researcher" movement has gathered more and more adherents. With the researches going further, a new paradigm appeared to enable English teachers to develop their own understanding of their own practices, and to turn their practice into a form of research. Goodman (1983) points out the development of teachers' personal theories of education should get from the experiences of their own reflection in action. McNiff (1993) thinks that "E-externalized" inquires are those conducted by one person into the practices of others. An "I-internalized" inquiry is conducted by the individual into her own practices. Self-reflection, self-direction and self-concept of one's own actions are once more emphasized to think of creative ideas, either privately or through discussion with others.

In an "I-inquiry" the purpose of research is to explain what "I", the practitioner, am doing. Its position is personal. "My" practice is an outcome of "my" thought, and "my" improved practice is an outcome of "my" improved understanding. The most important thing is that "I" can improve "my" thinking and "my" practice (an improvement in my actions). In this view, English teaching as researching aims to encourage the development of personal understanding that will lead to an improved form of practice.

The view of pedagogy makes English teachers responsible for discovering their own problems for the development of their professional expertise. Widdowson refers that outside research, whether descriptive, experimental or speculative, cannot therefore be directly transformed to the classroom context. It does have, however, a crucial role to play in two respects, theoretically and methodologically. Theoretically, it can serve as a source of ideas and insights, which are of potential relevance for the formulation of principles. It can provide model or example of what is involved in critical inquiry, of how intuition can be subjected to conceptual and empirical evaluation. It can raise consciousness of the whole process of continuing self-appraisal.

It should be considerably stressed that the relationship between teaching as learning and teaching as researching in English teacher development is a continuously interactive one. Learning can provide the opportunity for the testing and assimilation of researching, while researching can provide the analytic and conceptual apparatus for thinking about learning.

In ELT curriculum design and textbook reform provide English teachers with their professional development. In addition teacher training and education would foster English teacher development. Nevertheless language teachers in China have fewer chances in improving their professions. Language knowledge is overstated, resulting in concerning more about language teaching itself. They pay little attention to language teaching innovations including the combination of teacher education and practice. During the process of teaching, they are not critical of their self-concept, self-observation and self-assessment in teacher thinking completely. Overall language teaching cannot satisfy the needs of the development of society.

At present ELT is in urgent need with its characteristics of importance and specialty. Fullan and Hargreaves (1992) regard the effective implementation which consists of alterations in curriculum materials, instructional practices and behaviors on the part of teachers involved in given innovations. Put it more simply, successful change involves learning how to do something new. As such the process of implementation is essentially a learning process. Thus when it is linked to specific innovations, teacher development and implementation goes hand in hand. How can language teachers adopt a wider and more professionally focused frame of reference? One-step English teachers can take is to approach educational decision more formally and to attempt to get answers from the educational research that already has been carried out. By implementing procedures that are thoroughly grounded in educational research, English teachers not only increase the learning possibilities for students but also advance teaching as a professional endeavor. The contents, which should be acquired well about by English teachers, are as follows:

(1) To know well about modern linguistics and language teaching theories including philosophy of education, educational psychology, educational sociology, educational planning, comparative education, curriculum, educational technology.

(2) To learn well about discourse analysis, social linguistics, educational linguistics, psychological linguistics, pragmatics and applied linguistics.

(3) To contact closely with the second language acquisition, syllabus design textbooks assessment, self-performance evaluation, classroom observation, communicative methodology, testing and computer-assisted teaching.

(4) To operate effectively about teaching design learning requirement analysis, learning difference analysis, learning strategies analysis, teaching design management.

Teacher learning usually is the process of learning which consists of two processes, training and education. Training is the process of learning a sequence of programmed behaviors. Training is also the application of knowledge that provides English teachers with a set of procedures that will guide their work-related behaviors. Education is the process of helping an individual understand and interpret knowledge. Education emphasizes acquiring sound reasoning processes rather than learning a body of several facts. Teaching techniques can be improved by training because these activities are capable of being programmed. However English teachers have responsibilities that, in most respects, require education rather than training. Both training and education of teachers will serve not only to help their professional development, but also, in a very important and fundamental way, to tie the behaviors with the students learning. To become a professional is to reach beyond oneself and to arrive at the satisfactory destination of education and development.

The study of teacher thinking has significant meanings on teacher development especially in European and American universities. Teacher development would enrich and broaden the theory and practice of teacher thinking. Their relationship is reciprocal and supportive.

Theory ofteacher development is based on the recognition of the characteristics of teaching activities, which define the theory of teacher thinking. Firstly teaching activities are the reflections of social development. Secondly teaching activities are the effective ways for society's expectations for education. Thirdly teaching activities are the necessary processes for English teachers' professional development. Therefore researches on teaching activities are essential prerequisite for teacher thinking. In theory and practice of ELT the process of teaching activities is emphasized to observe teachers and students' relationship, position and autonomy in teaching. The principles and theories can be also applied in ELT teacher education. Especially recognizing the importance of teaching activities would be essential for English language teachers' professional development.

2 – 5 **ELT in UK**

2 – 6 **ELT in U. S.**

Teacher thinking is formed and set up through teaching activities, which foster English teachers' professional development. McNiff perceives that development is a transformational process. A person may hold certain views and sometimes make dogmatic assertions about them. However when he/she represents these views for public scrutiny and criticism, he/she may change his mind about them. Because of several influences by engaging in the analytic process of writing which focuses his thought more precisely; or by the feedback from other people as they criticize his work; or in the light of the own developing experience etc. Specifically for English language teachers, their development is rooted in their classroom performance and activities. Firstly the process of teaching is the process of activities, in which teachers and students encourage and support each other. Secondly the process of teaching is the process of social interaction. Thirdly teaching activities are the processes of changing. The factors that play influences on teaching activities are highlighted that aims, tasks, contents and methods of teaching activities would transform each other.

Marton (1994) points out ELT teacher development involves teachers in investigating the ways in which their students are disposed to learn the purposes for which they are learning. It involves teachers in exploring their own dispositions on the one hand and in their working environment to obtain more factors that are external on the other hand. It also involves, however, teachers identifying their own assumptions about the nature of language and of learning and teaching. It involves them in examining and developing their "experiential" knowledge (knowledge of language classroom) and "received" knowledge (knowledge of theories of language and the psychology of language learning). He also points out (1994) teaching activities could encourage English teachers to question and evaluate their assumptions, their awareness and their knowledge, and ultimately to modify these activities.

It is assumed that the research of teacher thinking and ELT teacher development could be centered on the teaching processes, through which the two aspects would be formed and achieved. To be adequate, accurate and systematic, researches of teacher thinking and teacher development should be integrated with the research of philosophy, morality, sociology, pedagogy and so on, which will make teacher beliefs and internalization possible and English teaching effective.

2.3 Corpus-based online Teaching and Evaluation in European and American Universities

Since Bologna Process corpus construction and research develops quickly in European and American Universities. The application of corpus technology in the field of language education teaching is also increasing widely and deeply. The application of corpus teaching is mainly reflected in two aspects. One is direct application, including the corpus knowledge, teaching how to use corpus to research, using corpus teaching, etc. Another is the indirect application, which is mainly based on corpus compiling dictionaries, grammar books and textbooks which are based on the corpus of target language or description and analysis of learners' interlanguage or linguistic features. Because of the large amount of information corpus teaching plays a unique role in the field of English teaching, and some domestic normal colleges also tried using corpus in teacher education.

2.3.1 Corpus Development in European and American Universities

In recent years the development of corpus teaching tends to be wider in use. At the same time some new statistical language model also begins to emerge. The construction and development of European and American corpus can be divided into three stages. The first stage is the manually corpus phase. This phase mainly refers to the 1950s. This stage of corpus construction mainly includes lexicography, grammar study for the purpose of corpus which is written for the purpose of English teaching and e-learning library with the purpose of language study.

The second phase is computerized corpus phase. This stage mainly refers to the 1980s, which marks the corpus transition from computer age to computerized age. Then the milestone is Quirk who announced the establishment of the Survey of English Usage (SEU) corpus. The style of the project is designed to collect a large number of different subject's corpora in British spoken and written English based on the system description. At this stage there are establishments of the SEU Corpus, Brown Corpus, London-Lund Corpus. Moreover the establishment of Computer Corpus, which overcomes time-consuming to collect language materials and makes Corpus linguistics into an undisputed status, it also gives a new meaning to Corpus. The establishment of the three corpora, of course, is just a start which needs to be perfected, for example, the database is not enough, the use of computer retrieval are still not strong enough to consult statistics. So far European and American computer programs have combined to obtain the required information after Bologna Process.

In the end of 1990 the construction of corpus ushered in a new phase, which is known as a new generation of corpus. This stage to COBUILD Corpus, whether KWIC (Key Word in Context) or retrieving statistical methods, has obvious improvement. It mainly adopted a new KDEM (Kurzweil Data Entry Machine) photoelectric symbol recognition technology, which makes the Corpus of coding and editing to be free from heavy manual input, greatly accelerates the Corpus annotation processing in European and American universities. The Corpus in this period carries out contains 500 million words, which contains 15 million words spoken corpora; it has become one of the largest Corpus in European and American universities.

After Bologna Process some corpus as BCET (Birmingham Collection of English Texts) corpus has been established, which has a capacity of 7.3 million words. In the 2000s, the scale of corpus entered into a period of rapid growth. Completed in 1994 the British National Corpus (BNC) has as many as 100 million words. It is by far the most representative of contemporary English information database. The fundamental reason why this period of corpus develops in such a rapid pace is that the emergence of the development of computer machine-readable corpus. Some other corpus as LINDSEI Corpus (Louvain International Database of Spoken English Interlanguage) and PELCRA Corpus (Polish and English Language Corpora for Research and Application) have been constructed in Belgium and Poland.

2.3.2 Application of Corpus in ETL

Over the past 30 years corpus was not only used in the study of language, but it also obtained the application in language teaching. Collins English corpus began in the 1980s which is mainly used in dictionary compilation of a large-scale corpus. According to corpus compilation, Collins press has published more than one dictionary, which includes the explained words, expressions, examples of cited language completely based on the corpus as well as English teaching and learning. Tim Johns, Tony DuMley Evaus and Philip Iiug firstly used it in the study of grammar and vocabulary words index (Concordance). It is one of the most basic corpus that employs analysis and takes students as the center. Let students find words in classroom by looking at a large number of corpus Data collocation, rules of grammar and pragmatic characteristics in order to cultivate students' ability of autonomous learning. Today we call it the interaction between students and corpus Data-Driven Learning, the establishment of the Data Driven Learning environment is oriented toward the classroom teaching. In addition the application of words index has played a positive role in the process of English teaching. Dieter MinMt tried to use the corpus to study design-teaching syllabus, teaching materials and created to use corpus driving the repository for the use of textbook editors and English teachers.

After 1990s the application of Corpus in English teaching has been rapid development in European and American universities. Researchers find that there is great difference between the actual English and English teaching material. Therefore they decide to change the contents of the textbooks and base on Corpus study first. Hence a set of complete series of textbooks is written based on Corpus analysis. This series of textbooks are based and compiled entirely on Cambridge International Corpus findings. AWL (Academic Word List) is designed based on common design of AFL (Academic Formulas List), which contains the high frequency of Academic vocabulary. In a word corpus studies influence the design of English syllabus, which effectively improves the teaching of Academic English in European and American Universities.

Since 21st century more and more English teachers begin to use Corpus in English teaching. English teachers can design exercises through Corpus retrieval software, students can also be based on online corpora for autonomous learning. For instance using online Corpus will enable English teachers design the gestalt exercises and practice through the Corpus, through which students can provide a series of vocabulary based on word retrieval to study the word formation, meaning and collocation etc. The MICUSP (Michigan Corpus of Academic Spoken English) belong to American Corpus which can also be used to help English teachers develop and perfect Academic English course by analyzing characteristics of academic English. Besides it can be used for students to study academic English learning resources. Gavioli suggested in 2001 that English teachers should not put emphasis on data classification, on the contrary, they should let students watch index line, the characteristics of the repeated words. In 2006 Gavioli provides examples of data driven learning activities for students from economics, which mainly includes the marketing professional vocabulary and emphasizes the collocation of keywords and phrases in practice.

2.3.3 Application of Corpus in Chinese ELT Pedagogy

The application of English teaching corpus research in China began in 1980s. Professor Huang Renjie and Yang Huizhong in 1982 built the corpus JDEST (Jiao Da English for Science and Technology) with the capacity of 1 million words, which collected 10,2000 science and technology words in the field of professional English text. In 1987 GPEC (Guangzhou Petroleum English Corpus) is built with capacity of 410,000 words and consists of 700 professional English.

Since the 1990s the construction of Corpus and its application research has been in rapid development. Some typical Corpus are respectively built with CLEC (Chinese Learner English Corpus), such as CSCEC (Chinese Students Communicative English Corpus), STC (Science and Technology Corpus), BLC (British Literature Corpus), etc. The first Chinese Learner English Corpus includes a collection of junior and senior middle school students, college English and professional English writings that are more than one hundred words in each writings with all the words in the syntactic tagging and speech errors.

SWECCL (Spoken and Written English Corpus of Chinese Learners) is the first English majors students' oral language Corpus in China, which contains more than 1000 Spoken English speech samples, 1 million words of phonetic transcription in the text as well as 1 million words of sample written compositions. Another corpus is COLSEC (College Learners' Spoken English Corpus) which contains 700, 000 words, including pronunciation, intonation, word wheel, discourse structure such as students' oral English information. Chinese research is trying to evaluate the curative effect of different corpus with 1 million words and consists of two parts, composition and translation.

PACCEL (Parallel Corpus of Chinese EFL Learners) Corpus is divided into two sub-categories: interpreting Parallel Corpus and translation Parallel Corpus. The completion of the corpus of English teaching research and reform in China has played a significant role in promoting ELT, which provides detailed information at the same time as well as the research on the rules of English teaching and textbook compilation. At the same time writings and teaching materials are published one after another based on corpus. Fudan university press published "21st Century College English" in 1999; Foreign Language Teaching and Research Press published "New Horizon College English" in 2003. The two sets of corpus-based writing teaching textbooks are not only convenient for college English teachers and students, but more important it laid a good foundation for application of corpus in ELT in China study. Chinese Universities has gradually absorbed European and American corpus in ELT pedagogy especially after Bologna Process.

2.3.4 Corpus in ELT Development

Future researchers in European and American universities start to consider how to make better use of corpus in English teaching. First researchers should pay more attention to the analysis of English teachers' actual demand and consider how to give them better help on teacher education. Researchers should launch more towards teaching corpus resources and provide basic training on the Internet. Once English teachers receive training, the knowledge they learned can be applied to teaching in that they will design their own teaching materials. Secondly English teachers should pay more attention to the actual needs of students' learning and different needs of learners based on different special corpus.

In addition the rapid growth of corpus will provide a good supporting role for the teaching with the rapid development of corpus research meanwhile the application of corpus in English teaching research will continue to deepen and expand. In the future European and American corpus can be used for teaching evaluation, providing truthful and accurate reference data for teaching evaluation and giving a relatively objective evaluation results. Definitely it has become a new trend in English teaching. Moreover it will certainly grow rapidly in Bologna Process.

Research priority of English corpus is to build a large-scale corpus through multistage processing. The corpus will contain at least millions of words to cover a variety of subject from the original text. Then through the automatic word parsing, such as part-of-speech tagging, syntactic structure analysis and tagging, semantic words can be processed easily. With a different processing level, language knowledge base will contain different annotation information in which a large number of useful statistics can be extracted.

Corpus will not only be applied to grammar teaching and vocabulary teaching, it can also be used in many teaching areas such as language testing, outline writing, teaching evaluation, discourse analysis, interlanguage studies and so on. With its systematic, scientific and rational characteristics, more and more ELT teachers begin to favor corpus and it gradually shows its important role in ELT teaching. At last we come to see that there are some problems in corpus-based ELT teaching such as the choice of the corpus, money problems and so on. To solve these problems still needs continued efforts of English educators. The application of corpus in English teaching is bound to achieve its target both in European and American universities after Bologna Process, which will influence the other parts of the world.

Bibliography

[1] Beauchamp, G. A. Curriculum Theory. Illinois: F. E. Peacock Publishers, 2001.

[2] Bowman, C. L. Comparison of Peer Coaching Versus Traditional Supervisions Effects. The Journal of Educational Research, Vol. 93. No. 4, 2000.

[3] Crystal, D. and Johnson, K. Applied Language Studies: Materials and Methods in ELT (eds.) Oxford: Blackwell Publishers Ltd., 1993.

[4] Edge, J. Cooperative Development. London: Longman, 1992.

[5] Fullan, M. and Hargreaves, A. Teacher Development and Educational Change. In Fullan, M. and Hargreaves, A. (eds.), Teacher Development and Educational Change. London: The Falmer Press, 2002.

[6] Fullan, M. and Hargreaves, A. Teacher Development and Education Change. London: The Falmer Press, 1992.

[7] Glasser, W. Control Theory in the Classroom. New York: Harper & Row, 1986.

[8] Goodman, K. S. Psycholinguistic Universals in the Reading Process. New York: Holt, Rinehart & Winston Inc. , 1983.

[9] Harmer, J. The Practice of English Language Teaching. London: Longman press, 1991.

[10] Joyce. B. and Shower, B. Student Achievement through Staff Development. New York: Longman, 2008.

[11] Leithwood, K. A. The Principal's Role in Teacher Development. London: The Falmer Press Neff, 1992.

[12] Marton, F. On the Structure of Teachers' Awareness. In I. Carlgren, G. Handal and S. Yaage (eds.), Teachers' Minds and Actions: Research on Teachers' Thinking and Practice. London: Falmer Press, 1994.

[13] McNiff, J. Action Research: Principles and Practice. New York: Macmillan Educational Ltd. , 1993.

[14] Nunan, D. Understanding Language Classrooms. New York: Prentice Hall, 1989.

[15] Stallings, J. A. School Achievements Effects and Staff Development: What Are Some Critical Factors? Paper presented at the annual meeting of American Educational Research Association, 2009.

[16] Stenbhouse, L. An Introduction to Curriculum Research and Development. London: Heinemann, 1975.

[17] Wajuryb, R. Classroom Observation Task: A Resource Book for Language Teachers and Trainers. Cambridge: Cambridge University Press, 1999.

[18] Widdowson, H. G. The Incentive Value of Theory in Teacher Education. ELT Journal, 2001 (3).

[19] 傅道春:《教师组织行为》,上海教育出版社 1993 年版。

[20] 吴宗杰:《行动研究:外语师资教育新途径》,《外语教学与研究》1995 年第 2 期。

[21] 吴欣:《行动研究:英语教师职业发展的重要途径》,《西南师范大学学报》1996 年第 2 期。

[22] 杨启亮：《试论教师道德的内在价值》，《江苏教育研究》1997年第4期。

注　　解

1. 欧盟委员会（European Commission）：简称欧委会，是欧洲联盟的常设执行机构，也是欧盟唯一有权起草法令的机构。欧盟委员会的任务在《欧洲联盟条约》221条及以下得到规定其具有主动权，可以建议提出法律文件，并为欧洲议会和欧盟理事会准备这些法律文件。在法律提案还没有获得决议的情况下，欧盟委员会可以随时撤回其法律提案。作为欧盟执行机构，其负责欧盟各项法律文件（指令、条例、决定）的具体贯彻执行，以及预算和项目的执行，它和欧洲法院一起保障共同体法律切实被遵守。作为欧共体在国际舞台的代表，其下设有教育和文化司负责欧洲大学教育的相关事务。

2. 劳伦斯·斯滕豪斯（Lawrence Stenhouse）：英国著名的课程理论家，在教育研究和探讨课程的设计发展方面做出了卓越贡献。同时，他还是东英吉利大学应用教育研究中心的创始人之一。他在进行了大量的理论研究并吸收了英国许多课程编制的实践经验的基础上，提出了著名的"过程模式"课程理论。劳伦斯·斯滕豪斯在从事"过程模式"研究之时，曾对泰勒的"目标模式"做了详细分析和批判。

3. 双语平行语料库（Bilingual Parallel Corpus）：指两种语言以上的语料库，分为平行语料库和对照语料库两种。平行语料库指库中的两种或多种文本互相是对方的译文，因此可以用于翻译或者机器翻译研究；对照语料库中两种或多种语言的文本不构成对译关系，只是领域相同，主题相近，通常只能用于两种或多种语言的对比，博洛尼亚进程后双语平行语料库在欧美大学英语教师教育中非常盛行。

4. 语料库教学（Corpus-based Teaching）：欧美大学英语教师利用语料库描写语言词汇、语法结构，探索词汇和语法层次，说明特殊语境下语言的不同用法并进行语言特征的频率统计，解释句型和意义间的关系，近十年来这方面研究和实践取得了不少成果，为英语语言教学提供了极有价值的资源和信息。

Chapter Three Task Research and ELT Development

3.1 Task Research

Task research is a kind of special research method widely used in Bologna Process. The earliest use is in the forties of the 20th century by collier J. Collier and Lewin K. Lewin advocating its use in social science research. Task research is applied in the field of ELT education, which is advocated by S. M. Corey, the head of the Horace-Mann-Lincoln Institute of School Experimentation at Columbia University in the 1950s. ELT researchers have paid more attention to task research since 1970s.

3.1.1 Definition of Task Research

In view of the definition of task research, there are various viewpoints. The original concept is sometime attributed to Kurt Lewin in which task research is the term that describes the integration of task (Implementing a plan) with research (Developing an understanding of the effectiveness of this implementation). His vision of task research was as an alternative to the norms of decontextualized research; instead of focusing on surveys and statistical methods, task research's purpose is to improve social formations by involving participants in a cyclical process of fact-finding, planning, exploratory and evaluation.

3 - 1 **Task Research Classroom**

3 - 2 **Task-based Teaching**

Stephen Corey, the head of the Horace-Mann-Lincoln Institute of School Experimentation at Columbia University in the 1950s, is a leading voice for promoting task research education in the USA. He and his colleagues at the Institute collaborated extensively with school districts and teachers across the USA in conducting studies of various teaching problems. Corey produces a number of papers and books on task research education that discusses what he refers to as the method of "Cooperative Task Research" and reports on various studies conducted in US universities that are supported by his Institute.

Wilf Carr and Stephen Kemmis made an important contribution to the development of task research theory and methodology by locating it within the framework of critical theory, which is in particular related to the work of task observation classroom. Task research became a means of realizing the ideal of democratizing the power in universities and institutions. Hence task researchers, working collaboratively, would be able to create "ideal speech situations" in which communication between individuals would be free and open, unconstrained by considerations of power and status. Carr and Kemmis's book described a task vision for the future rather than a current reality.

McNiff proposes that task research is a form of self-reflective inquiry undertaken by participants (teachers, students or principals, for example) in social (including educational) situations in order to improve the rationality and justice of (a) their understanding of these practices, and (b) the situations (and institutions) in which these practices are carried out.

A most frequently cited definition in the field of language teaching is one by Kemmis and McTaggart, which reveals the nature, purpose, method and scope of task research in Bologna Process.

3.1.2 Characteristics of Task Research

Generally speaking task research has four characteristics, they are respectively collaboration of teachers, researchers and participants in which the purpose is to solve given task, change given situation and develop ELT theory.

Task research can be also characterized as being:

(1) Integration: it is the way that conducted as part of a teacher's normal daily practice;

(2) Reflection: it is a process which alternates between plan implementation and critical reflection;

(3) Flexibleness: it means that methods, data and interpretation are refines in the light of the teaching and understanding process;

(4) Action: a process designed to generate change in small steps;

(5) Relevance: it means to meet the needs of teachers and/or their students;

(6) Cycle: it involves a number of cycles with each clarifying issue lead-

ing to a deeper understanding and more meaningful outcomes;

(7) Focus: it refers to focuses on a single issue of teaching and learning improvement;

(8) Collaboration: it refers that teachers and leaders work together to improve student outcomes;

(9) Plan: it is an organized approach to solve given task;

(10) Learning: it is the simultaneous construction of new knowledge by teachers about their practice.

3.1.3 Functions of Task Research

The linking of the terms "Task" and "Research" highlights the essential feature of the method in which it tries out ideas in practice as a means of improvement and as a means of increasing knowledge about the curriculum, teaching and learning. The result is improvement on what happens in the classroom and extra-curricular activities, and better articulation and justification of the educational rational of what goes on task research which provides a way of working which links theory and practice into the whole task teaching and learning process.

Hence it is the descriptive case study of a particular classroom, group of learners, or even a single learner if it is initiated by a task which is supported by data and interpretation and carried out by a practitioner investigating aspects in his or her own context and situation.

Task research explains that ELT teachers should involve themselves in task research on the basis of the assertion that most teachers would like to develop their expertise progressively as they continue in their chosen occupation.

With the Bologna Process there have been a trend that more and more ELT teachers in European and American universities involves themselves in task research experience. They begin to develop perspective of a spiral of steps for task research and turn the concept into the basis for an adequate and coherent educational science. They agree with the basic idea of task-reflective steps in cycles, but they elaborate that ELT teachers in university classroom should have collaborators to work with.

Task Research often conjures a picture in people's minds of academics working in isolation. As distinct from academic research, it involves in participating in an ongoing testing and monitoring of improvements in ELT practice. ELT teachers work in a collaborative way to identify issues in their organization and develop processes for improvement. In ELT education, task research is also known as teacher research. It is one method ELT teachers use for improvement in both their practice and their students' learning outcomes. The central function of task research is positive educational change that can be summarized as:

— To help ELT teachers to implement inquiry method;

— To help solve needs of their own teaching task and situation;

— To help ELT teachers to take action towards the classroom problems.

3.2 Procedures and Processes

It has been controversial in task research field that whether task research is a method or a methodology. In the literature about task research, some scholars view that task research is not a researching method, but a methodology while some consider that, it is an educational research method, concerning related methodology. Although it is understood as a research method, it has its own research techniques, and the basic process or model.

3.2.1 Task-based Procedure in ELT

Many ELT teachers in European and American universities have used "steps", "circle" and "spiral of cycles" to design the general process of task research. In the perspectives, the plan of task research begins with a general idea. Here, "the general idea" actually refers to a "problem domain" or "subject" in the research fields.

The first step is to use simple way to examine the objective and get reconnaissance or fact-finding in the situation. The second step is to perform the identified "overall plan". The third step is to observe the process of action, which has four functions:

(1) Preparation: it will show previously expected goals;

(2) Observation: it is to provide researchers with learning opportunity,

namely enhance new insights;

(3) Plan: it is to lay a reliable basis for the next plan;

(4) Revision: it is to provide foundations for amending "overall plan".

The fourth step is to redesign process of plan, execution, and observation in order to evaluate the efficacy of the execution of the second step, to provide a rational basis for the design of the third step, and the "overall plan" to make possible changes.

Lewin's "Spiral of cycles" provides a good example for the future task researchers, although it is not perfect. In 1980s, Kemmis (1981) modified Lewin's "spiral of cycles", and constitutes "plan-action-observation-reflection-re-plan... " which is known as "Kemmis Program".

It can be explained in three ways: first, analysis, fact-finding and conceptualization about task problems; planning of action programs, executing them and then more fact-finding or evaluation; finally a repetition of this whole circle of activities.

Through the spirals of these activities, task research creates conditions under which learning communities may be established, i. e. communities of enquiries committed to learning about and understanding the problems and effects of their own strategic task, and the improvement of this strategic task in practice, which is illustrated in Figure 1:

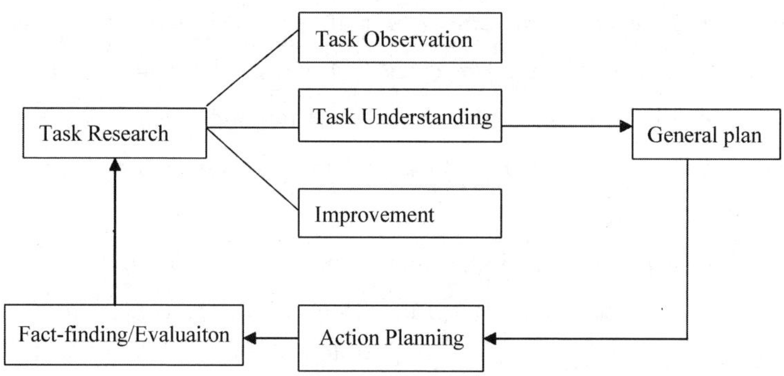

Figure 3 – 3 **Task-based Research Model in ELT**

There are three steps in ELT Task-based Research. The first step is to make the general plan. In above model it also begins with a general plan. In the field of action, normally, a classroom teacher puts forward a general idea about what is happening now. The teacher describes the situation and then gets reconnaissance through discussing and negotiating to explore opportunities, assess possibilities and examine constraints.

Then we come to the next step: the action step. During this step, ELT teachers' role is designing and evaluating task since teaching and learning is required to revise general plan to evaluate the action's effect.

The third step is fact-finding or evaluation. This step is to circle the second step. ELT teachers still monitor and evaluate the effect in understanding and learning task.

3.2.2 Task-based Research Process in ELT

From above it can be seen that Task-based Research Model in ELT in a sense reflects some characteristics of action research: (1) it emphasizes the learning task in action and highlights ELT teachers' research status, rejecting the traditional research model that is far from education practice. (2) Here the process "Task-Plan-Action-Reflection-Evaluation-Replan......" is an endless exploration. (3) "Reflection" interprets ELT teacher as a task researcher. (4) "Evaluation" highlights the importance of "fact-finding", which is easy to be neglected in task-based research process. (5) The structure of spiral cycle expresses the improvement and development of task-based research.

We can make a a summary about the process of task-based research. Firstly it puts forward a general idea to get reconnaissance. Then it gives an overall plan to conduct task in monitoring and reconnaissance. Finally one can revise the overall plan to make it amended which shapes a new general idea and continue the spiral cycle.

This is an endless circle. Task-based actions are all about monitoring and reconnaissance process. ELT teachers can revise and evaluate the plan to monitor task-based research so as to get reconnaissance through this circle.

We describe the procedure of TR as the systematic collection and analysis of data relating to the improvement of some aspect of professional practice. Furthermore several other features of TR in European and American universities are put forward in Bologna Process, which states task-based research should be collaborative or team-based. Others suggest academic publication or at least sharing of the process and results in the task-based investigation somehow. It has also been suggested that the same stringent requirements of validity, reliability and verification for conventional research should also apply to task-based research. Finally ELT teachers should make sense of differences between task-based research and other traditional types.

At large TR is focused on individual or small-group professional practice and is not much concerning with making general statements. It is therefore more "user-friendly" in that it may make little use of statistical techniques.

3.3 Principles of Task-based Research

3.3.1 Origin and Development of TR

Task-based Research (TR) is the process of systematically collecting research data on an ongoing system relevant to some objectives, goals, or the need of that system. However these data will be fed back into the system based both on the data and hypotheses while ELT teachers may evaluate the task-based results by collecting and analyzing more data. Despite some controversy about the origins of task-based research, it has been considered a distinctive form of problem-solving method since the early 1980s. Kurt Lewin is generally regarded as one of the pioneers (Checkland, 1981; Argyris etal., 1985). And he advocates to use the term "Task-based Research" to refer to a specific research approach in which teachers generate new social knowledge in a social system while attempting to change it at the same time (Peters and Robinson, 1984).

A distinctive emphasis on task-based research has also been perceived by University of Lund in Sweden as a groundbreaking method to deal with sociological and psychological problems arising from teaching pedagogy in Bologna Process.

Although early literature on task-based research suggests that it grew from a desire of researchers to deal with important social problems shortly after its early development in the late 1980s, task-based research began to be used by practitioners in large scales to deal with intra-organizational teaching and learning problems. Thus task-based research is defined as a critical collaborative inquiry by reflective practitioners, who are accountable in making the results of their public and self-evaluative inquiry in teaching and learning practice, which is engaged in participative problem solving and professional development in European and American universities in Bologna Process.

Initially task-based research model is only applied to be descriptive rather than being predictive because the deeper involvement of practitioners are influenced by contextual and environmental factors due to time constraints when they study a small number of instances of particular events. However, as the number of task-based research studies which are carried out on a similar topic increases, the descriptive models are then integrated into more general and predictive models and eventually led to grand theories in ELT fields in that task-based research has been applied. Terms including participatory research, task-based learning, praxis research, participatory inquiry, collaborative inquiry, action inquiry and cooperative inquiry etc. are also used in ELT literature. The term "TR" is regarded as an umbrella term that includes several traditions of theory and practice. Today applications of task-based research can be identified in a number of relevant fields including organizational management, community development, education target, organization development, and participatory evaluation etc.

The term task-based research (TR) is generally believed to be coined in 1980S by professors at Oxford University, Barcelona University and MIT in Bologna Process in order to solve teaching and research problems of ELT, later TR is gradually described as a comparative research on the conditions and effects of various forms of educational tasks leading to social action in that it uses a spiral steps, each of which is composed of a circle of task, planning, action, evaluation and fact-finding about the result of teaching and learning process. Now ELT teachers not only define the content of TR but explain the way of its application.

The earliest use TR in the field of ELT appeared at Columbia University. ELT professors are believed that educators involved in research and application would bring about changes in whatever work they are engaged. Valuable changes happen in everyday teaching practices rather than generalizations to a broader audience and ELT teachers will benefit collaboration between teachers and researchers in practice. However TR is being attacked as little more than common sense and the work of amateurs.

This period is described by Burns (2005) as one of technical-scientific and problem-solving, not drawing on scientific and quantitative methods. TR inUK emerged in the 1980s in the context of the school-based curriculum reform movement (Elliott, 2010). By the late 1980s, however, interest in TR waned as experiments with research designs and quantitative data collection which became the norm later.

3－4 **TR Classroom in UK**

A second generation of TR, practical and illustrative, utilizing case study and description was contributing to educational and curriculum theory by the 1990s (Burns, 2005). TR was again emphasized to emerge and hold great value. For example, professors in European and American universities began to advocate the concept of teacher-as-researcher somehow. These educational practitioners questioned the applicability of traditional scientific research designs and methodologies as a means to solve education issues.

A third generation of TR called-critical emancipatory, drawing on critical, constructivist and dialectical methodologies began in 21st century in Bologna Process. So far TR is often recognized as a tool for professional development and university reform as well for it is bringing a greater focus on ELT teachers than before. The characteristics of TR are shown in different perspectives and developmental stages. It is so inspiring that ELT teachers and researchers search for truths of TR. The closer they are to it, the more benefits ELT teachers will enjoy and the more changes will take place. TR is realizing the essence of ELT education.

Normally speaking, there are three stages of task-based research in the whole process, namely, Technical TR, Practical TR and Critical TR. Their philosophical bases are different. Technical TR comes from natural sciences, Practical TR is from Hermeneutics, and Critical TR is from Critical theory. Thus we can see they are three stages of TR. The problem is concluded from natural sciences. Then from Hermeneutics perspective, people started to practice it. The last stage is from Critical theory to check its effects in task-based research.

Their natures of realities are different as well. For Technical TR, it is measurable. While practical TR is multiple, holistic and constructed, critical TR is inter-related with social and contextual structures.

They are also three periods of task-based research from the nature of problem-solving perspective. Technical TR is pre-defined period with the problem posing. Practical TR is the problem solving period with a defined context. Critical TR is a period with a defined context in relation to emerging values, the problem-solving evaluation period.

In status of knowledge perspective, Technical TR is separate and deductive. Practical TR is inductive and theory producing stage. For Critical TR, it is with characteristics of inductive theory producing in terms of emancipator and participatory together.

From the nature of understanding, Technical TR means that events are explained in terms of real causes and simultaneous effects. Practical TR refers to events described in terms of interaction between the external context and individual thinking. For Critical TR, it means that events are understood in terms of social and contextual constraints to improved conditions.

Increasingly growing interest in TR can be seen from the number of books, papers, articles and presentations in the public domain. A glance through the program of the American Educational Research Association or the British Educational Research Association reveals that presentations on task-based research and related topics were rare in 1990s whereas they are increasing quickly after 21st century in Bologna Process.

In his view on TR, Elliott (2010) has tried to distinguish this school of research from others such as "Task-based Inquiry" or "Reflective Teaching" on the grounds that research places teachers under an obligation to render the insights they have gained from an inquiry in some publicly accessible form. He argues that TR involves teachers' making and creating educationally worthwhile changes in their classroom and other learning environment.

Carr and Kemmis (1986) stated that TR is simply a form of self-reflective enquiry undertaken by participants in social situation in order to improve the rationality and justice of their own practices, their understanding of these practices, and the situations in which the practices are carried out. They polish this definition twenty years later in other words task-based research aims to change practices, people's understandings of their practices, and the conditions under which they practice.

From above we come to provide a useful summary on TR. Within all these definitions there are four basic themes: task empowerment of participants; collaboration through participation; acquisition of knowledge and social change. As a result task-based research is seen as a means towards creating meaning and understanding in problematic social situations and improving the quality of human interactions and practices within those situations. When we analyses TR from professional, personal and social dimensions after carefully studying the literature on ELT task-based research and various strands of relevant social research we may assert that TR offers a way to understand and thereby use task-based research as a means not solely for knowledge generation, but for personal and professional development, and for contributions to teaching action.

The development and definition of TR discussed above manifest that task-based research of ELT is assumed to lead to some changes initiated from either teachers-based or students-based activities in modern and social contexts. It obviously deviates from traditional quantitative forms, for instance, its participants comprise teachers, social workers, administrators in the name of practitioners instead of subjects, who may go through a series of phases (Task-based Research Cycle), to identify problematic settings, and work collaboratively with their colleagues to pursue professional excellence by themselves. The changes that happen to them will eventually have great impact on the setting they work in. People may wonder, however, why teachers are deprived of accountability to do research, which is questioned all the time in and out ELT educational field. The main answer is that ELT teachers are accessible to task-based research procedure.

3.3.2 Teachers as Researchers

Globalization and marketization have stimulated teachers to make choices either striving to empower themselves to make and create change through task-based research, or simply handing responsibility for change over educational reform. Empowered teachers are likely to initiate ideas to bring about their desired outcome and improved outcomes from their students. ELT teachers can make a crucial difference in this aspect. If the changes are initiated by outsiders, such as policy maker and educational managers in some cases, English teaching are decontextualized and therefore impractical so that ELT teachers may appear resistant in its implementation. It may be clarified more explicitly that ELT teachers are likely to ignore the theories produced by researchers on the grounds that they are practically irrelevant somehow since they can't connect themselves with their ordinary common sense experience. Many of ELT teachers try to transfer themselves to researchers in European and American universities after 21st century.

The term "teacher-as-researcher" can be discerned that the core of classical paradigm of educational research seeks to present results or conclusions as products of a technical research process and thus to override teacher judgment and research judgment. It may be further asserted that what the classical research procedure offers to teachers is not conclusions to accept but hypotheses that need testing. Hence teacher-as-researcher can markedly improve the art of teaching process. Teacher-as-researcher process will involve two aspects, namely offering hypotheses (i. e. tentative conclusions) whose application can be verified because the teacher can test them in the classroom; offering descriptions of cases or retrospective generalizations about cases sufficiently rich in detail to provide a comparative context in which to better judge one's own case.

It is clearly shown that teacher-as-researcher is much different from traditional research results with practices of teachers. The emergence of teacher-as-researcher movement is to provide an alternative research tradition or paradigm, to generate practical theory opposed to pure, traditional theory, and to bridge the theory-practice division. It is now widely recognized that teacher-as-researcher process has unique insights into practice that are simply not available to researchers who come from outside therefore professional knowledge is hereby an essential component of understanding any educational practice.

3.3.3 Reflective Teachers in Task-based Research

It is generally acknowledged that Dewey is the first person to define reflection, a process or activity that is central to developing practices. Reflection is predominantly associated with acts of cognition that are linked to learning "how" rather than learning "about" or "what". However, the term "reflective teachers" makes practitioner known to the professionals since 1990s. It is argued that ELT practitioners should be critically reflective. ELT researchers come up with the following definition that reflection is the ability to think and consider experiences, perceptions, ideas (values and beliefs etc.) with a view to the discovery of new relations or the drawings of conclusion for the guidance of future action in task-based research. In other words, reflection enables individuals to make sense of their lived experiences through examining such experiences in context. Reflection, although a cornerstone of ELT practice, is not the only skill which is needed in teaching and learning process.

3 – 5 **Reflective Teaching in University of Barcelona**

As for reflective practice, it is more than just a thoughtful practice. It is the process of turning thoughtful practice into a potential learning situation which may help to modify and change approaches to practice in ELT process. ELT reflective practice involves the synthesis of self-awareness, reflection and critical thinking.

3.4 Task-based Observation

Classroom is a useful place to observe, examine and evaluate ELT teachers' performance and students' practice. Through the observation in classroom, ELT teachers will become better informed about their strategies used in class teaching. Besides classroom observation and research will do effective work for ELT teachers' self-development and self-evaluation. Classroom observation, as a main criterion of task-based research, covers a wide range of possible research techniques and also has specific and immediate outcome which can be directly related to practice in ELT teacher's own context. As is indicated from above classroom observation tasks seek to provide stimulus ideas for ways of exploring one's own teaching by observing other teachers and classrooms in action, or by having one's own classroom teaching observed for the purpose of continued learning and exploration.

3.4.1 Observation Tasks

An observation task in ELT is a focused activity to work on while observing a lesson in process. It focuses on one or a small member of aspects of teaching or learning and requires the observer to collect data or information from the actual lesson, such as the language a teacher uses when giving instructions or the patterns of interaction that emerge in a lesson. An observer may watch a lesson alone or with others; a number of observers may watch different lessons for the same reason or in the case of a video or demonstration lesson; many observers may be involved simultaneously. The relevant data may later be collected for purposes of analysis and interpretation.

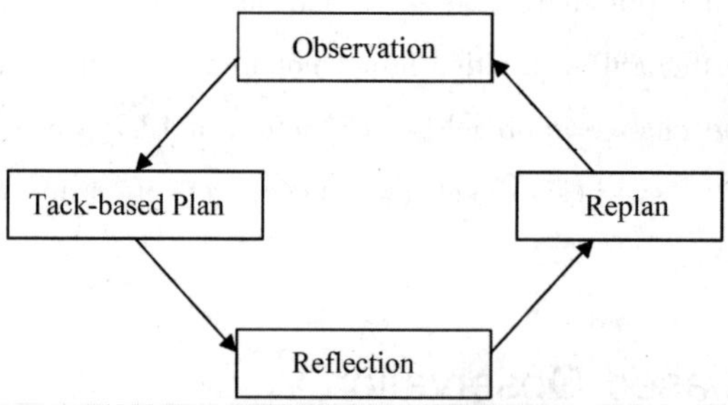

3 – 6 **Task-based Observation**

The tasks should be designed to give ELT teachers:

(1) A way of observing that provides both focus and clarity;

(2) A means of collecting classroom-based data and information about teaching;

(3) A greater understanding of teaching and learning to be more informed and systematic;

(4) A channel of developing awareness;

(5) A method of developing skills of evaluating theory according to practice;

(6) A thinking of developing pedagogic skills and the ability to evaluate

practice.

According to above model we will come to see that tasks will form the basis for ELT teachers to devise new ones to fill the gaps as they are perceived in any particular circumstances. The following classification is to present explicit contents about the aim, focus and activity of task-based observation.

Task-based observation in ELT is aimed:

(1) To benefit transformation of knowledge;

(2) To improve collaborative professionalism;

(3) To construct personal knowledge;

(4) To identify problems;

(5) To focus on self-inquiry;

(6) To emphasize on learners' self-direction.

Main content of ELT in task-based observation is focused on:

(1) Comments made by learners, teachers, experts;

(2) Lesson plans;

(3) Schemes of work;

(4) Course materials;

(5) Samples;

(6) Questionnaires;

(7) Recordings about discussions, statements;

(8) Questions about the participants' belief.

ELT activities in task-based observation are perceived as:

(1) Reading (texts, materials, statements);

(2) Listening (opinions, tapes);

(3) Watching (activity, presentation);

(4) Writing (ideas, summaries, questionnaires);

(5) Writing (communicating, exchanging, asking questions);

(6) Teaching (techniques, skill used);

(7) Selecting (materials, data);

(8) Comparing (two lessons, two people, groups);

(9) Recording (interviews).

There are different aspects and types of classroom tasks in different context.

It is reported that ELT teacher's workshop offers the following criteria: time waiting; repairing techniques; fun; questioning; materials; student-teacher interaction; scope of student response; class organization; lesson objectives; student and teacher talking; control and initiative; context for language practice; variety of activities; interaction between students; lesson cohesion; teacher's spoken language; eliciting techniques; evaluation etc.

3.4.2 Process of Task-based Observation

The new teaching curriculum in European and American universities is another top-down task-based policy to be implemented at all levels in many countries. A system of ELT faculty development is advised to be established to guarantee the high quality of teaching. The policy makers are aware that the quality of ELT teachers is the key to the improvement of the teaching quality and to the development of College English program. Colleges and universities are aimed to build a faculty team with a good structure of age, educational backgrounds and professional titles, lay emphasis on the training and development of ELT teachers, encourage them to conduct teaching and research with a focus on the improvement of teaching quality, create conditions for them to carry out relevant activities in various forms, and promote effective cooperation among them, hence they will better adapt themselves to the new teaching mode in Bologna Process. Meanwhile opportunities should be created so that ELT teachers can engage themselves in advanced studies, thus ensuring sustainable improvement in their academic performance and methods of teaching.

The new developing trend in European and American universities sounds quite sensible, comprehensive and instructive with regard to its consideration of ELT training and research activities in various forms, even ELT teachers cooperation is advocated among different universities or countries. The modern teacher education theories and practices are reflected and manifested in ELT teachers training. What ELT teachers are expected is to work out their own working model based on individual context. Without clear workable guidelines and detailed instructions, without room for discussion and articulation of disputes, without consideration of implementation feasibilities in differentiated contexts ELT teachers will feel quite puzzled as to where to go. The speculated assumptions is that ELT teachers are taken for granted to have been equipped with all these needed theories, knowledge and abilities, which is exactly what to be coped with their task-based training project. We thus envisage five-step actions to bridge the gap of ELT teachers' discrepancies according to a typical task-based research cycles: (1) Task-based Planning; (2) Reflection; (3) Observation; (4) Evaluation, which is likely to better implement the new curriculum more successfully. Here is process of task-based observation in ELT teaching class:

Step 1: Talking shop: ELT teachers as participants meet to discuss the feasibility of implementing a learner-cantered classroom teaching, and its possible outcomes via answering and discussing the task-based questionnaire, which investigates ELT teachers' perceptions on classroom teaching/learning, research, new teaching theories such as communicative approaches.

Step 2: Self-reflection: Participants individually reflect on and write down their own present practices and classroom monitoring strategies.

Step 3: Meeting: ELT teachers meet again and share their views on the planned changes to the learner-centered classroom.

Step 4: Observation: ELT teachers observe a real English class demonstrated by one of them with learner-centered teaching model.

Step 5: Micro-teaching: ELT teachers are allocated into small groups to conduct Micro-teaching. Each group shares their teaching strategies with other small groups for the use in the classroom setting. On implementation in the following new semester, these teachers will meet again to continue reflecting, planning, monitoring and evaluating as they work towards achieving the initial objectives.

Task-based Observation is the main activity that is completed in the process of observation. It serves for the evaluation of ELT classroom teaching. First task should be meaningful, not imaginary since authenticity task will arouse teachers' desire for learning and exploring knowledge. Second task should not be too small or trivial in general, as can be divided into several subtasks. Only in this way can ELT teachers get a larger space on exploration and innovation. Third task will cover skills to learn, but the way to complete the task can be varied in that formation of the results can be rich and colorful. In addition task should be open to give ELT teachers who participate in observing and evaluating class some space to create. At last it should also be operable and appropriate, that is to say, task should be appropriate to learners.

Task-based Research (TR) can make up for the inadequacy of language teaching. It encourages ELT teachers to be aware of their own practice, to be critical of their practice and to be prepared to change it on large-scale as well as small-scale inquiries. Through the inquiries and reflection on their own practices, ELT teachers will acquire development theoretically, practically and professionally.

Task-based research is a form of research that enables ELT teachers to develop their own understanding of their own practice, and to turn their practice into a form of research. It is a process of reflective cycle to develop themselves in skills as a language teacher or skills of evaluating theory according to practice and sensitivity to learners. Hence the fixed and unchangeable teaching can not adapt themselves to the current educational reforms. Task-based research provides ELT teachers with good opportunities to adjust themselves to the change, especially in Bologna Process. To some extent, task-based research motivates and fosters ELT teacher development for knowledge inquiries, which is a sound enlightenment to us.

Bibliography

[1] Argyris, C., Putnam, R., and Smith, D. M. Action Science. San Francisco: Jossey-Bass, 1985.

[2] Burns, A. Task-based Research: An Evolving Paradigm? Language Teaching, 2005 (38).

[3] Carr, W. Kemmis, S. Becoming Critical: Education, knowledge and Research. London: Falmer Press, 1986.

[4] Checkland, P. Systems Thinking & Systems Practice. Chichester: Wley, 1981.

[5] Chen, X. M. Action Research-An Approach for Teachers to be Researchers. Henan Education, 2004 (9).

[6] Edwards, C & Willis, J. Teachers Exploring Tasks in English Language Teaching. Beijing: Higher Education Press, 2009.

[7] Elliot J. Collecting, Analyzing and Reporting Data in Task Research: Some Methods and Techniques. Handout, 2010.

[8] Elliot, J. Educational Action Research and the Teacher. Retrieved from http://www.uea.ac.uk/edu/ddncl/. April 19, 2010.

[9] Ernie Stringer. Action Research in Education. Upper Saddle River: Prentice Hall, 2004.

[10] Fox, W M. An Interview with Eric Trist, Father of the Sociotechnical Systems Approach. J. Appl. Behav. Sci. 26 (2), 1990.

[11] French, W. andBell, C. Organization Development: Behavioral Science Interventions for Organization Improvement (6th ed.). Upper Saddle River: Prentice Hall, 1999.

[12] Kirkwood, M & Christie, D. The Role of Teacher Research in Continuing Professional Development. British Journal of Education Studies, 2006 (4).

[13] Peters, M and Robinson. The Origins and Status of Task Research. Applied Animal Behaviour Science, 20 (2), 1984.

注　　解

1. 任务型教学研究（Task-based Research）：是指教师通过引导语言学习者在课堂上完成任务来进行的教学。这是20世纪80年代在欧美国家兴起的一种强调“在做中学”（Learning by Doing）的语言教学方法，是交际教学法的发展，在世界语言教育界引起了人们的广泛注意。这种“用语言做事”（Doing Things with Language）的教学理论也逐渐引入中国的大中小英语课堂教学研究，是中国外语课程教学改革的一个走向。该理论认为：掌握语言大多是在活动中使用语言的结果，而不是单纯训练语言技能和学习语言知识的结果。在教学活动中，教师应当围绕特定的交际和语言项目，设计出具体的、可操作的任务，学生通过表达、沟通、交涉、解释、询问等各种语言活动形式来完成任务，以达到学习和掌握语言的目的。任务型教学法是吸收了以往多种教学法的优点而形成的，它和其他的教学法并不排斥。

2. 研究型教师（Teachers as Researchers）：研究型教师就是具有较强的研究意识和研究能力的教师。研究型教师是教师成长的高级阶段，他不同于纯粹的教育理论研究者，因为他有丰富的教学经验；他也不同于一般的有经验的教师，因为他对教育教学有强烈的研究意识并在教育研究方面形成了自己的特色。从事英语教育研究不仅是英语教师基于教学任务认识、分析和解决复杂的教育问题和提高教育教学质量的需要，而且也是改变英语教师专业生活方式，实现英语教师专业成长的必由路径。

3. 观课任务（Task-based Observation）：指观察一堂课是怎样开展的过程中所关注的一种活动，观课任务是课堂参与者基于任务教学相互提供教学信息，共同收集和感受课堂信息，在充分拥有信息的基础上，围绕共同关心的问题进行对话和反思，以改进教学的教师研修活动。这项活动聚焦在教或学的某一个或某些方面，要求观察者收集来自实际课堂的数据和信息，例如通过观课任务发现一堂课形成交际模型时教师所使用的语言特征等等。

Chapter Four Cooperative Work for Teacher Development

Self-development is the center of teacher development. Traditionally teachers' professional training, education and performance in class are always one's own behaviors. His development is in his own hands. With or without official training and education as a teacher, he can understand what he is going to do or he is not going to do.

It seems likely, however, that this point of view can not be argued or even criticized. But as a member of a school, a society and a culture, one can survive only by contacting, communicating and negotiating with other people. The same situation is true for teaching and learning. The emphasis on individuality does not mean that a teacher should teach in isolation, which holds him back and makes him ill-informed. If a teacher always depends on isolated, subjective and individual experiences sharing with no one, he will restrict his abilities to develop as a qualified teacher. Self-development of one's own professional needs shared understandings of students, colleagues and experts in English language learning, teaching and research.

According to the dictionaries, the word "colleague" can be explained as follows: assistant, associate, companion, fellow worker, partner, teammate, workmate. These words provide us with rich imagination that working together and helping each other are a kind of pleasant experiences and attitude towards the work and life. Edge (1992) feels that cooperative work is a way of working together with someone in order to become a better teacher in his own terms. Classroom research through cooperative work with others can:

—Understand teachers' experiences and opinions.

—Enrich them the opinions and experiences of others.

—Modify their teaching strategies in the light of shared understandings.

—Undertake sustained and supportive academic work.

—Understand the sufficient system of the language to prepare language teaching materials on a second basis.

—Have a chance to escape from simple and egocentric subjectivity.

4.1 Cooperative Principles

With ELT innovation going furthering, teachers must learn to apply pedagogical theory to classroom functions. A particular issue is the need for close supervision and guidance when they participate in field-based ELT. It is universally accepted that cooperative teaching and learning are recognized as an alternative model. Teams of teachers regularly observe each other to provide suggestions, assistance, and support.

The cooperative work also provides opportunities to refine teaching skill through immediate feedback and through experimentation with teaching strategies as a result of the evaluation. Furthermore, during the process of cooperation, teachers collaborate to develop a shared language, forums to test new ideas about teaching, and ultimately, expertise.

4.1.1 Experiential Language Learning model

Cooperative teaching and learning belong to experiential language learning model, which focuses on internal motivation and cooperative consciousness to initiate the participants' self-direction, self-development and self-evaluation by the form of team teaching and group learning. Kolb appoints that in experiential learning and researching, immediate personal experience is seen as the focal point for learning, giving life, texture, and subjective personal meanings to abstract concepts and at the same time providing a concrete, publicly shared reference point for testing the implications and validity of ideas created during the teaching and learning process. The importance of personal experiences for the growth of personality is similarly prominent in humanistic psychology. Rogers refers that the individual's self-concept is a social product that is shaped gradually through interaction with the environment. A positive self-regard and an unconditional acceptance promote the development of a healthy self-concept by the significant others. It is also pointed out that the process of change is characterized by a widening range of human experiences: an awareness of one's own feelings as well as openness to new experiences, tolerance, a basic trust in others, and an ability to listen to them empathetically and perceive their feelings. Kolb presents us a clear outline of how "experiential" learning model functions in the circle.

In the past decades, the educational context changes profoundly, as a result of developments in pedagogical theories, it may become necessary for teachers to consider deeply about the English language teaching for the purpose of new development. Educational beliefs and attitude towards teaching should be shifted from the tradition of delivering knowledge to the "experiential" model which is aimed to (a) facilitate personal growth; (b) help learners adapt to social change; (c) take account of differences in learning ability; (d) respond to learner needs and practical pedagogical considerations.

Teachers who act as both learners and researchers for their own professional development initiate the critical awareness of personal practice to be available to their students as to themselves. The introduction of experiential model in cooperative teaching and learning is defined to present a pleasant atmosphere of shared partnership, a common purpose and a joint management among themselves.

4.1.2 Conditions for Cooperation

When two or a getup of people sit and talk together, certain norms are followed. This is even more likely to occur when we converse across cultural boundaries, even if we appear to share a common language. So how to bridge two sides of different aspects for the smooth communication always remains a problem. There are many complaints from inside and outside communities about the qualities of dialogue, conversation and communication. Creating peaceful circumstances can make the cooperation active, associative and acceptable. It is of value that shaping a way of interacting that seems particularly useful when the aim is to encourage the Teacher Development.

Cooperative development depends totally on the idea of an agreement among people to work together for a certain period of time according to roles that they understand and agree on. As their work together continues, they may want to renegotiate the roles, but common understanding and agreement remain essential. The problem of cooperation among people lies at the very heart of some underlying attitudes on which cooperative development has to be based.

Like any form of cooperation, cooperative development requires a relationship of trust and confidentiality. In addition, three particular qualities must be presented in the interaction among the teachers and students. Respect, empathy and honesty are the cooperative bases. Mutual respect is profound to cooperative work. Participants accept each other's opinions, suggestions and evaluations without any prejudices and judging them according to one's own subjective values. Empathy is a kind of attitude, which infers how all of the members understand the classroom language learning and teaching completely. Workmates should try every chance to get into the world of each one to share each other's experiences end feelings. According to Edge (1992), it is something we aim to get better at, rather than expect to achieve totally. It is also something easier to experience than to understand or explain. For lack of honesty, how can you be genuine about your respect and empathy? Getting the most out of cooperative development depends on having colleagues you can reply and trust, because cooperative development can help colleagues develop mutual trust and reliability.

Cooperative work would seem to provide a good environment for discussions, comparisons and understandings of the specific language tasks. The teammates must obey to the cooperative principles. Each member should regard motivation and information gaps as the base of cooperation, because each one can make up the inadequacies in knowledge, information and competence from the collaborators. Crawford (1993) indicates that cooperative work should possess the following five characteristics:

(1) Collaborators must think it is necessary for them to cooperate finishing the task.

(2) Collaborators must communicate and interact with each other by summaries, explanations and descriptions about their former experiential knowledge.

(3) Collaborators must practice their social skills involving a basic trust in the teammates' willingness and ability to cope with the various learning tasks. On the basis of such a relationship, they can be given increasing amounts of initiative in undertaking the task, choosing the contents and assessing their work.

(4) Collaborators must learn their respective language materials and help others learn the language materials.

(5) Collaborators must be given chances to analyze how their group would work and how they would make full use of social techniques. There are great differences in personality, motivation, emotion, social experience, cognitive styles, intellectual level and interest, which present them the information gap with the basis of cooperation.

Cooperative work seems to provide a classroom environment in which the needs of learning, teaching and research can be met in a way that is beneficial for both academic achievement and the development of the teachers' social and teaching skills.

4.1.3 Forms for Cooperation

Classroom work is goal-oriented, aiming to achieve common goals in teaching and learning. The work to achieve learning goals can be operated so as to promote individual learning, competition and cooperation among the participants. Individual work focuses on working at one's own pace and at one's own speed. His achievements are independent of himself. His progression is unrelated to what others do. Competitive work stresses the competition to judge who is the best one. In such a circumstance, there are little motivation and intention to work together. In cooperative work, participants are encouraged to work together to arrive at the common goals. They have the same responsibilities and mutual benefit to create a positively interdependent circumstance among themselves. Obviously, cooperative work is more concerned by researchers and teachers, because it can encourage academic achievement, personal growth and social development.

Collaboration among teachers is aimed to improve personal academic growth and enhance the levels of students' communicative competence. There are many ways for teachers to conduct cooperative work such as preparing lessons collectively, giving lectures cooperatively and attending class each other.

Teachers can have shared understandings to improve preparing lessons collectively. We all know that, even though the textbooks are the same, different teachers have the different information gap in points of view and understandings. Teachers' cooperation has repeatedly demonstrated that broadening mind and sharing each other's intelligence can be obtained at reasonable costs with such method. There are advantages as follows:

—To enhance levels of the effectiveness of preparing lessons collectively.

—To enforce communications of knowledge and emotion among teachers.

—To stimulate teachers' self-development.

—To foster spirits of collaboration in wider context of the school and community.

Common lecturing is, conducted on the basis of collaboratively preparing lessons collectively, with the characteristics of two teachers lecturing one class, one teacher lecturing several classes under the observation and guidance of other teachers in class and out of class. Common lecturing can expand students' range of academic experiences and professional expertise by understanding shared performance of different teachers in school.

Attending class is also one of the effective ways for teachers' cooperation. The feed back after class can offer teachers' methods and techniques in class performance. Cooperative work between teachers and students is aimed to lead students to greater autonomy and motivate their active thinking. Cooperation in class can be conducted by teachers' lecturing, teachers and students discussing under the teacher's guidance and direction. Teacher is the director and designer by whom the activities and tasks in class are guided. The students are the main actors to pursue self-access activities with the help of the teachers. Harmer (1991) thinks that the best teachers are those who can consider carefully about how to manage the class effectively.

Cooperation between teachers and students can improve the performance of self-concept, self-direction and self-access for teachers' personal growth and students' learning. This kind of cooperation ideally involves the following features:

—To allow greater progression in self-awareness, cognition and intelligence.

—To permit students to progress cooperatively at their pace including a self-correction through discussion.

—To force students to practice language skills and strategies

During the process of cooperation in classroom performance and activities, teachers' lecturing plays an important role for the success of classroom teaching and learning. The lecturing contents and resources must be sufficient to provide students with a large quantity of knowledge. Firstly, teacher should give lessons intensively and encourage students to obtain the broadest information with the limited time. Secondly, teacher is the organizer of the classroom, in which he is expected to bring along how to think and how to learn for the students. He should be always aware that students can be motivated by teacher's designing of all kinds of interesting activities for enhancing the communicative competence. But the designing of the programmers must be considered particularly as follows:

(1) He must lead the students obtaining the communicative competence.

(2) He must obey the students' experiential knowledge.

(3) He must direct the students in thinking actively with the combinations of background knowledge, learning experiences and language strategies.

Cooperative work among the students will offer students a wide choice of learning materials and the possibility of becoming more self-reliant and less teacher dependent. Cooperation among the students can be performed in pairs and small groups in class and outside the class. Harmer (1991) also considers group studies for learners provide each other with potentialities and energies. For example, members of one group may write the same assigned subject composition or the different one. Before writing, they discuss the theme, structure, and style of the subject, making every effort to express oneself.

One of the members will write the draft for all the members to revise and correct. Obviously, discussion and assessment about the first draft will enlarge a broader sense of thinking, making writing become a social act. In a word, cooperative work will show the language teachers how to apply the theoretical principles to the practice and improve the teachers' professional development through observations of the classroom activities. Also it affords the learners' opportunities to practice the learning of English in an open way so that they will emerge as confident and competent language learners.

4.2 Collaboration among ELT Teachers

Teacher Development involves teachers in exploring their own dispositions on the one hand and more external factors in their working environments on the other hand. Professional competence involves, however, teachers identifying their own assumptions about the nature of language and of learning and teaching in examining and developing their "experiential" knowledge and extending their "received" knowledge. Tasks as focus will encourage teachers to question and evaluate their assumptions, their awareness and their knowledge. For personal growth, language teachers should be constantly required to use their experiences to text out theories, and to use theories to test out their assumptions through cooperative work with other colleagues.

4.2.1 Peer Coaching

Teachers who join the teachers' groups are usually motivated by a desire for self- improvement. Cooperative work offers an assessable but disciplined framework which teachers can use to draw on their own experiences and understandings of their own situations. It is a style of interaction designed to allow teachers to collaborate for the widely accepted goal of autonomous development.

Social process is the basis of development. Through the social interaction, new knowledge is produced when people interpret, transform and internalize their thoughts and ideas. Peer coaching allows individuals to develop their own perspective and to play influences on others. According to Joyce and Showers (1988), they classify the four training components for the preparation for peer coaching:

—Developing understandings of the rational for peer coaching

—Demonstrations

—Simulated practice

—Analysis of the simulations

Peer coaching should be accompanied with teaching skills to contribute to the clarity of instruction. Allright (1988) suggests six skills for effects of peer coaching: (a) accepting feelings, (b) informing students of lesson objectives, (c) repeating important points, (d) using examples, (e) asking questions, (f) praising or criticizing, (g) providing practice opportunities.

Through peer coaching, language teachers can understand the effectiveness of each supervision model on the development of skills. They can evaluate the contents of cooperative work including discussions, analysis, ideas and materials swapped, and advice given and taken. They can also ascertain whether the field experiences of peer coaching work in language teaching and learning for arriving at the aims they have set.

4 – 1 **Collaborative Teaching in University of Oxford**

4 – 2 **ELT in University of Princeton**

4.2.2 Task as Focus

Task is chosen as a focus because there is evidence that task is a systematic unit in both language teaching and learning. Without the systematic unit, it is impossible to make some assessment of proposals for relating the teaching to the learning. Crooks proposes that task as a major unit of analysis shows its potential strength and utility throughout all educational research and design (Crookes 1986).

For the field experiment, the teachers are assigned in pairs, along with a cooperating teacher who observes each other teaching. Before conducting the tasks, the peer will be informed under the guidance of the teacher about their actions used in teaching Bowman (2000) suggests:

—Understanding the relationship of one idea to others in the same and in different subject areas.

—Contemplating, selecting, and planning instructional activities.

—Applying teaching acts.

—Assessing students' understandings and misunderstandings.

—Reflecting on the teaching and Teaming in a lesson.

The following communication describes peer interaction during discussions with a teacher working as an observer. Sample 1:

Peer Coach: Can you list some reading skills?

Peer Teaching: Skimming, scanning, receptive reading and intensive reading.

Peer Coach: How do you consider about the elements or factors for effective reading?

Peer Teaching: I' ll study carefully about the needs, interests and abilities of the learners.

Observer: Yeah, the reading materials in which they are interested always motivate the learners.

Peer Coach: How do you enable the students to involve themselves into reading quickly?

Peer Teaching: There are many methods such as teaching them to look for unfamiliar words and topic sentences.

Peer Coach: Furthermore, we can ask them to use the context to work out the meaning of unfamiliar words, or translate some of the contents mentally.

Observer: How do you think about the background knowledge?

Peer Teaching: Background knowledge is very important to effective reading. As teachers, they should provide the students with a lot of knowledge concerning history, nature, geography, politics and culture in western countries.

Peer Coach: I agree with you. The appropriate input based on the students' practical learning conditions will work for improving their effective reading. Now, can you explain in details about intensive reading, scanning, receptive reading and skimming?

Peer Teaching: Reading intensively means paying more attention to the exact words such as reading poetry and legal contracts. Novels, magazine or newspaper articles are usually read receptively. Scanning is a visual skill. It forces reader to read quickly to find useful words for answering the questions. Skimming also requires reader to look through the material quickly and find out the gist of something.

Observer: Right. Students may need practice in choosing in what way to approach a particular text and in using the different skills of intensive reading, receptive reading, scanning and skimming. The choice of these skills will depend on factors such as the nature of the text and the purpose in reading it.

Post-conferences among the peer coach, teaching peer and observer are usually conducted before the teaching peer presents simulated lessons to his teammates or gives lessons in an authentic context to his students. They can get benefits from the post-conferences because:

(1) Students receive feedback related to their teaching not only from persons in authority but also from a peer.

(2) Feedback is invariably immediate, that is, in every case post-conferences between peer groups occur as soon as the lesson ends, which is also the case when the teacher (observer, supervisor) observes.

(3) Post-conferences are always based on direct observation of instruction.

4.2.3 Evaluation of Peer Coaching

When you think of the best teacher and the worst teacher you ever had, how do you make the choice? Is it the judgement based on how much the teacher seems to know about the subject matter? Or is it important to know that the characteristics of the teachers are visible in the classroom performance. These characteristics can be observed and evaluated by researchers, colleagues and teammates. Through evaluation, the teachers improve their teaching and profession. As Medley, Coker and Soar suggest:

Evaluation of teachers focuses on the teaching act itself. Performance evaluation is designed to evaluate the teacher on the basis of the quality of teaching he provides in a specific setting with a particular class, in a particular school, in a particular community. It is, of course, process bases-based on the behavior of the teacher in the setting.

(Medley, Coker and Soar 1984: 21)

Professional action demonstrates language teachers' capabilities as classroom practitioners. Of course, classroom performance is concentrated, but also their participation in supervision and self-evaluation are included. Wallace (1991) appoints that it is important to note that professional act assessment is formative, as well as summative. Observation schedules should be devised not only to give a reliable and valid assessment of the trainee's performance, but also to act as a diagnostic instrument to improve that performance.

After the cooperative work, the teachers might have their evaluations about their teaching performance based on the tasks and classroom activities. Evaluation of the peer coaching will take place in several ways:

(1) At the end of the cooperation, every teacher is given a basic questionnaire to find out how the teachers think of the lessons, their language skills and the styles of teaching.

(2) The teachers are also asked to fill out questionnaires asking for comments and criticism of the peer coaching.

(3) The teacher (observer) is asked to write internal reports on the peer coaching and also on the individual's performance in teaching.

(4) Similar report outlining any problems and suggestions for fostering teachers' professional development.

(5) There is an end-of-session meeting among these teachers discussing about the new form of peer coach different from traditional supervision effects.

Just as there are different methods and styles of teaching and learning, a variety of modes of assessment can also be chosen to present reasonable judges on the teachers' teaching performance. Wallace (1991) summarizes the assignments, which are generally used; (a) exercise, (b) presentation, (c) essay, (d) review, (e) contract, (f) project, (g) guided reading assignment, (h) workbook, (i) dissertation.

In above discussion, I only put forward some suggestions of how peer coaching is conducted to strengthen ELT. According to the discussion, assistance from peers can be extremely productive in achieving field experience goals. Peer coaching based on tasks performance can receive feedback immediately from teaching, peers and observers. Obviously, they can be very quick to obtain information about their instructional activities.

In language teaching, teachers, learners and researchers can collaborate to experiment with the methods of organizing teaching and learning. Through the cooperative work, they can promote a philosophy of cooperation rather than competition and create an environment in which they can learn from each other. Besides, cooperative teaching permits teachers to take advantages of individual teacher strength and motivates creativity because teachers know that they must teach for their colleagues as well as for their learners. In a word, cooperative work encourages language teachers to observe and reflect on their professional practice. The various engagements conducted by teachers with learners, colleagues and researchers will change our beliefs of ELT by understanding the nature of teacher decision making, and strategies for their self-awareness and self-evaluation, ultimately for the Teacher Development.

4.3 Some Current Models in ELT

The concept of Teacher Development makes us know about the approaches of research and practice. Obviously, ELT and Teacher Development can not be separated completely. The integration of three aspects will make teaching remarkable and productive. Wallace (1991) classifies the three models into: the craft model, the applied science model and the reflective model for ELT. Above all, reflection should be focused on to provide the language teachers with new thoughts and creative ideas.

4.3.1 The Craft Model

The so-called craft model regards the teacher as a craftsman. The young trainee learns by imitating the expert's techniques. He is instructed and guided by the expert, whose craft and expertise are passed on from generation to generation. From the mid-term in the 1940's to the present time, this point of view has fostered extensive influence on language teaching. The young teachers learn from the experienced teachers, whose teaching behaviors and performance are considered as kinds of models. Especially in pre-service teachers' teaching practice they do every teaching all based on the teacher guidance and direction. Firstly, they observe what and how the teachers teach in class. Secondly, they prepare the lessons and present simulated lessons and give lectures to their students by following their teachers' instructions and advice. Thirdly, after the teaching practice, their supervisors present their evaluations. Pennington (1990) points out that this kind of craft is basically conservative and traditional, depending on a comparatively stable society. In contemporary world, knowledge keeps on changing and developing. Teaching syllabus, methodology and situations also change and develop radically. In ten years' time, things will be very different from what they are now. The traditional teacher thinking and teaching methods can not be satisfied with the demands of the society. Both the theorists and teachers should think about how language curriculum, syllabus and language teaching reflect current views of language and of the processes underlying reading, listening, speaking, writing and translating skills.

Currently, research directed to these does not provide straightforward answers to questions about the feedback in development language skills. For this reason language teachers must operate the methodology issues on a case basis and evaluate within the constraints of the situation in which they are used. The reflection on the traditional teaching methods will present a valuable form of professional development.

4.3.2 The Applied Science Model

With the development of the modern pedagogy, linguistics and psychology, the new and creative researches and studies are applied in language teaching. The applied science model emerges accompanied by the consistent changes of theories. Objectively, the craft model still stands for the purpose of language teacher training, especially in some skills' training. The difference is that the teacher is not only regarded as the craftsman, but as a researcher in the applied science model. The applied science model is the most influential model of training the people into their professions. Wallace (1991) suggests that the applied science model is the traditional and probably still the most prevalent model underlying most training or education programs for the professions. This model derives its authority from the achievements of empirical science, particularly in the nineteenth and twentieth centuries.

Within this framework, practical knowledge of anything is simply a matter of relating the most appropriate means to whatever objectives have been decided on. The whole issue of the practice of a profession is therefore merely instrumental in its nature (Wallace 1991: 7).

Pennington points out that some educational theorists introduce the methods of the natural and scientific experiments into the language teaching. They try to justify the language teaching theoretical assumptions by strict and systematic observations of the classroom performance and activities. Foreign language theories always come from the disciplines of psycholinguistics and sociolinguistics. These considerations bring us creative and challenging view of teaching as applied sciences. It should be considered that the above theories are applied in language teaching directly. For example, the introduction of communicative approach has been considered extensively by both researchers and language teachers for ELT. The core of communicative approach is to improve learners' communicative competence, focusing on the fluency of their mastery of English language. Learners are centered in the teaching practices. Whereas; teachers are organizers, directors and assistants to help the students express themselves completely in discussions. The communicative approach aspire the researchers and teachers to recognize that the purpose of language teaching must be put at a more advanced level. They are encouraged to come to know the relevant relationship between the study of language and the application of language. In fact, the introduction of communicative approach has brought vitality and confidence to the English language teaching. Compared to the traditional teaching methods, it has its more advanced and positive sides to foster the language teachers' professional development. It is because of its instrumental and experimental characteristics that make people know the necessity and possibility of the innovations in language teaching.

But on the other hand, the opposed points of views also arise in the applied science model. Schon (1983) presents that the applied science model makes difference between the theorists and the practitioners. Usually, theory is admired as science and can not be criticized and doubted. So the practitioners always find themselves in an embarrassing situation that they put the theory into practice. When it fails in teaching activities, they can not find the better solutions whether they accept it or reject it. Indeed, almost by definition, as the professional science develops, it brings about changes in the practical element. However, these changes can be established only on experimental basis, and not by the practitioners themselves: White (1988) analyzes that practice driven by theory can not be believed, because practice itself shows its characteristics of complexity. Language teachers can not adopt these theories without any careful considerations and analysis.

Anyhow the applied science model contributes a lot to ELT. We must keep in mind that Teacher Development depends on the teachers themselves who improve their self-awareness by doing researches about their own practices in the classroom. They look for problems and find the solutions through the applications of new and creative teaching methods. The process of experiment and exploration in methodology is the process of Teacher Development.

4.3.3 The Reflective Model

1n western countries, the concept of reflection went back to John Dewey. He thought that reflection was a particular thinking and cognitive styles. He acquired the results by exploring, analyzing, observing and thinking about solving the problems. 'Reflective' model is basically put forward by the American sociologist Donald. A. Schon in his various writings, notably *The Reflective Practitioner: How Professionals Think in Action* (1983) and his later book *Educating the Reflective Practitioner* (1987). Schon develops Dewey's reflective philosophy, regarding that practice plays an essential part in teachers' professional development. He thinks the practitioners are more authoritative than the theorists and experts, for they have practices and experiences in the classroom. Frankly, the practitioners are busying doing teaching job, having no time to do research work. The educational theorists or the experts have no chances to do practical work in the classroom, only thinking of and imagining about some assumptions which are waiting for being justified or tested out. This is the almost complete separation between ELT researching on the one hand and practice on the other hand. Many practicing teachers might not be able to understand the more technical research articles. However educational researchers understand the frustrations and survival techniques in the classroom in an abstract way. Researchers can be contemptuous of teachers because "they seldom read". Teachers can be antipathetic to researchers because the latter are seen as refugees from the classroom. Stenhouse (1975) points out the point of view that teachers should regard them as researchers, being encouraged to do researches on their performance in the classroom. Nunan (1990) also suggests that educational experts and practicing teachers should work together to conduct the classroom research. Schon (1983) describes "know-in-action" in this way:

The workday life of the professional depends upon tacit knowing-in-action. Every competent practitioner can recognize the symptoms associated with a particular disease, peculiarities of a certain building site, irregularities of materials or structures—for which he cannot give a reasonably accurate or complete description. In his day-to-day practice he makes innumerable judgements of quality for which he cannot state the rules and procedures. Even when he makes conscious use of research-based theories and techniques, he is dependent on tacit recognitions. Judgements are skillful performances.

Wallace (1991) supplies that it is possible to leave these feelings or intentions either unexplored or unconsciously stored, or it is possible to reflect on them leading to the conscious development of insights into know-in-action. It is normal for professionals to reflect on their professional performance, particularly when it goes especially well or especially badly. They will probably ask themselves what goes wrong or why it goes so well. They will probably want to think about what to avoid in the future, what to repeat and so on.

Comprehensively, in terms of our human value, people develop individual strength according to their own interests and capabilities. For the practicing teachers, the purpose of ELT is to make teachers aware of the process of their own sense. The way to develop this process of sense is through critical reflection on their personal practices in teaching. If not enhancing the teachers' self-awareness and fostering their refinement of characteristics as teachers, it is impossible for them to develop in their profession.

4.4 Reflections on ELT

Kurt Lewin, a social psychologist, was keen to study social issues and also to provide people with an instrument of how to engage the teachers in their own inquiries into their own lives. He described action research as a spiral of steps. Each step had four stages: planning, acting, observing, and reflecting. It is believed that the spiral, through which teachers' communicative competence, language competence and methodological competence are enhanced, impresses most of the English language teachers. The following contents are concerned with offering specific methods and procedures of how to reflect or reflect on English teaching practice.

4.4.2 Key Elements in Reflection

"Received" knowledge and "experiential" knowledge are the important elements in language teachers' professional development. They offer basis and condition for reflection. 'Received' knowledge refers to facts, data, theories, etc. It is associated with the study of a particular profession. For example, if you want to be a language teacher, you should know well about the knowledge of the English language, linguistics, psychology of learning, psycholinguistics, sociolinguistics, educational management and administration, TEFL methodology and etc. Experiential knowledge, though we have discussed in the last chapter before, here refers to professional action or one's own practical experience. Experiential knowledge is usually related with one's professional actions. Glasser (1992) summarizes the functions of experiential knowledge in language teachers' professional development. It presents:

—Transformation of knowledge;

—Teacher as a learner among learners;

—Active participation in cooperative groups;

—Construction of personal knowledge;

—Organization of subject matter;

—Emphasis on teaching and learning skills, self-inquiry, social and communication skills;

—reflection on process, self-assessment.

So far these two elements have been discussed largely in isolation although some people regard that "received" knowledge input can be taught more experientially by using appropriate teaching skills. Anyhow, we should find ways to relate the subjects of "received" knowledge to teaching the experiences. The reflective model offers that making the relationship between 'received' knowledge and 'experiential' knowledge reciprocal, not one-side or one-way. The practicing teachers can reflect on the "received" knowledge in the light of classroom experience, and on the other hand, classroom experience can feed back into the "received" knowledge. Wallace (1991) gives us suggestions of how to relate these two sides together:

(1) Teaching practice can feed into the "received" knowledge and is also influenced by the experiential knowledge.

(2) Tutors delivering received knowledge input can meet with trainees to discuss about their school experience.

(3) The assessment of the "received" knowledge puts offer trainees an opportunity to apply the "received" knowledge in a school or classroom context.

(4) The tutors harmonize their input to see how these input relating to one another, as well as to teaching the experiences.

The "reflective cycle" is an effective way of relating reflection on "received" knowledge and "experiential" knowledge, which play a very important role in the language teachers' professional development. In the process of teaching performance, the teachers are met with problems and difficulties in, for example, how to motivate the students' interests and how to improve their awareness of self-direction, self-access and self-concept. At this time, the teachers can recall their relevant knowledge or experiences, which might encourage them to solve the problems. The reflection can take place before the teaching action, during the teaching action, of course, after the teaching action. For example, when you are teaching reading, you always do like this: (a) to teach vocabularies, (b) to underline the short expressions, (c) to explain grammatical points, (d) to ask the students to read the questions. When you grade their reading materials you find that they have made a lot of mistakes. Under the circumstances, you feel discouraged and criticize your students in class that they do not listen to your lecture attentively and read carefully. Through the reflection, you understand that you do not deliver reading techniques to your students such as the skills of intensive reading, receptive reading, scanning and skimming for effective and fast reading. In this particular teaching context, you pay more attention to the "received" knowledge in classroom performance but ignore the importance of the "experiential" knowledge. By means of reflection, you try to combine the two sides together and finally make your teaching productive.

"Received" knowledge and "experiential" knowledge are two significant dimensions. The reflective model works as a bridge to connect the two sides together. According to McNiff (1993), ELT does not mean a process of A→B→C... N, in which N is the ultimate and anything short of N is failure. But it is the creative process of $A < B < C$... N, in which values are realized in practice through the reflection on the "received" knowledge and the "experiential" knowledge.

4.4.3 Structures for Reflection

Reflection in teaching practice is a program that has influenced ELT and related research for more than a decade. Zeichner, a researcher on language teachers' reflection (1994) suggests establishing collaborative research communities, which implies research for teachers rather than about them. The following is about the practical example of the specific structures and instruments of a case study. It is designed specially by ELT teachers about what to reflect and how to reflect on the English language teaching.

(1) Collaborative Work

From a developing and changeable perspective in ELT, establishing collaborative research groups involves a process of ongoing professional development that sees language teachers as learners and researchers. They are challenged to improve the efficiency and relevance to give all the students an equal chance for their personal development. Furthermore, they have to respond in their teaching to changing educational demands. There are many strategies for establishing collaborative research groups. Action research, for example, focuses on the teacher as a researcher provides an effective tool for the language teachers' reflection on their teaching. Cooperating with others through action research can:

—offer an effective way to communicate.

—involve good suggestions and opinions.

—foster shared responsibilities.

—enhance social skills.

—allow greater progression in self-awareness, recognition and intelligence.

(2) Project

Changing English language teaching into reflective practice is one of the goals to seek to establish unanimous and supportive relationship among the teachers themselves. For example, the cooperative research group chooses the Communicative Approach. Problems and Thinking as the object for . research work. The teachers should be informed of the problems existed in communicative approach such as: (a) It breaks off grammatical teaching systems; (b) It cannot make up for the inadequacies of structural teaching approach; (c) It needs analysis, but language itself is complicated; (d) It is met with a lot of theoretical problems, which cannot solve the practical problems.

Once the problems are discovered, the participants would imagine solutions to solve the problems. These participants should attempt to formulate a strategy that would involve them in a joint research endeavor. They discuss, explore and analyze about the position of communicative approach in English language teaching.

4.4.4 Reflection on the project of a case study

(1) Theoretical Background

The participants in the group need theoretical guidance to reflect their pedagogical and didactic discomfort and to transform the latest discoveries and creative ideas into the practical teaching. For most language teachers, this kind of study would not just change roles, but change their teaching paradigm which can result in the successful practice, because the paradigm shift empowers teachers as reflective practitioners. Whitehead's view (1983) is that theory is an outcome of practice, and is part of an overall strategy of theorizing, which is a form of practice.

The teachers can ask themselves why the communicative approach is met with problems and difficulties in practice. Through the exploration and reflection on the theories related with the communicative approach, teachers would come to know that the communicative approach is formed based on the theories of semantic syllabus and notional-functional syllabus, which focus on speaking "what", furthermore on the students' communicative competence.

(2) Experiences and Findings

Experiences make us aware of what is going on and help us develop deeper insights into how the theory plays its role in practice. By recalling the "received" knowledge and "experiential" knowledge, the participants find why the communicative approach can not improve the learners' learning completely. To solve the problem, they attempt to combine the theory and practice together for further thinking

(3) Teachers' Voices

Establishing a reflective practice directs the teachers in exploring, analyzing, observing and thinking about the assumptions and also about how to make these assumptions applied in the practice. For example, how about combining the communicative approach with the traditional approach or how about introducing the two-stage approach by Wikins (1983), the ladder-spiral approach by Brumfit (1980), and the procedural approach by Prabhu (1978) into the communicative approach. All these teaching approaches are put forward by the theorists and researchers. The teachers might be encouraged to conduct teaching by the combination of theory and practice. They might say:

Teacher A:

The deeper understanding and recognition of the 'received' knowledge and "experiential" knowledge change my role as a teacher and my behavior.

Teacher B:

I am motivated by the inquiry method.

Teacher C:

I should spend much more studying theory.

Teacher D:

Indeed, I am reflecting. But I think the study changes my way of teaching.

Teacher E:

Generally, I become aware of how to do research work as a teacher.

(4) Personal Development and Growth

Through the researching and reflection on their group study, it will change teachers' teaching practice in various ways. Compared to their former patterns, their teaching will be more student-centered. They will be no longer transmitting contents of knowledge, but facilitating autonomous learning, which starts from the students' interests and everyday thinking. Obviously, personal development and growth will be fostered with the changing in teaching and in interaction with society, community and students.

(5) The Influence from the Project

The project of case study will give a general perspective for a pedagogical reflection. The reflection is situated on a practical level. On the one hand, it suggests a whole process of how to do research work. On the other hand, it makes a particular teacher be aware of his own rights as a teacher. If the teachers come to recognize that the student-oriented and activity-oriented way of teaching can be productive, conductive and effective in English language teaching, it will justify that the project of case study is satisfactory and acceptable. Reflective practice describes a goal not only for teachers' professional development, but also a process of change which is rooted in teachers' deep concerns about the effects and efforts of their instructional practice. Anyhow, reflection can take place before the event, during the event and after the event. It can also take place with only one person, or in peers and in groups.

ELT teachers arguably represent the most significant factor in any language teaching performance. As far as the "good language teacher" is concerned, it is often related to the students' good examination results. But the essential problem for ELT and Teacher Development is for teachers how to initiate students' motivation, attitude and interest in English studies. Nevertheless, despite the impossibility of precise measurement, as Crystal and Johnson (1993) suggests the "good language teacher":

—Knowledge of the language system;

—Good pronunciation;

—Qualification (Perhaps further training taken, or in-service development);

—Classroom performance;

—Evidence of being a good colleague;

—Length of time as a teacher;

—Ability to write teaching materials;

—Careful planning of lessons;

—Experience of a variety of teaching situations;

—Personal qualities;

—Publication;

—Knowledge of language theories;

—Wide vocabulary;

—Ability to manage a team of teaching.

Reflection in ELT is crucial because it is through the reflections on language teaching that teachers' perceptions and experiences are mediated, interpreted and realized for being "good language teachers". Comprehensively, reflection fosters the professional development in such aspects as the belief, values and characteristics of the language teachers.

Great changes have taken place in ELT over the last fifteen years in European and American universities since Bologna Process. These changes in turn have created new set of knowledge and advanced techniques that teachers need to acquire. A great many teachers have been trained and educated under the guidance of theories and practices in such aspects as action research, cooperative work, classroom observation and reflection in language teaching and learning. These trends, of course, are by no means the end but rather just the beginning of even more dramatic changes at a fast pace. We have to be prepared to meet the ongoing challenges in ELT Teachers' Development.

Bibliography

[1] Bowman, C. L. Comparison of Peer Coaching versus Traditional Supervisions Effects. The Journal of Educational Research, Vol. 93. No. 4, 2000.

[2] Crystal, D. and Johnson, K. Applied Language Studies: Materials and Methods in ELT (eds.). Oxford: Blackwell Publishers Ltd., 1993.

[3] Edge, J. Cooperative Development. London: Longman, 1992.

[4] Harmer, J. The Practice of English Language Teaching. London: Longman, 1991.

[5] Lewin, M. Educational Innovation in Developing Countries. New York: Macmillan Press LTD., 1991.

[6] Marton, F. On the Structure of Teachers Awareness. In I. Carlgren, G. Handal and S. Yaage (eds.), Teachers' Minds and Actions: Research on Teachers' Thinking and Practice. London: Falmer Press, 2004.

[7] McNiff, J. Action Research: Principles and Practice. New York: Macmillan Educational Ltd. Teaching as Learning: An Action Research Approach. London: Routledge, 1988.

[8] Medley, D. M., Coker, H. and Soar, R. S. Measurement-Based Evaluation of Teacher Performance: An Empirical Approach. London: Longman, 1984.

[9] Nunan, D. Understanding Language Classrooms. New York: Prentice Hall, 2000.

—1990. Action Research in the Language Classroom. In Richards, J. C. and Nunan, D (eds.). Second Language Teacher Education. Cambridge: CUP.

—1992. Collaborative Language Learning and Teaching. Cambridge: CUP.

—1992. Research Methods in Language Learning. Cambridge: CUP.

[10] Parrott, M. Tasks for Language Teachers: A Resource Book for Training and Development. Cambridge: CUP, 2003.

[11] Pennington, M. C. A Professional Development Focus for the Language Teaching Practicum. In Richard, J. C. and Nunan, D. Second Language Teacher Education. New York: Cambridge University Press, 1990.

[12] Prabhu, N. S. Second Language Pedagogy. Oxford: OUP, 2006.

[13] Richards, J. and Nunan, D. (eds.). Second Language Teacher Education. New York: Cambridge Press, 1990.

[14] Schon, D. A. The Reflective Practitioner. New York: Basic Books Inc., 2003.

[15] Sinclair, J. McH and Coulthard, M. Toward an Analysis of Discourse. Oxford: OUP, 2005.

[16] Stallings, J. A. School Achievements Effects and Staff Development:

What Are Some Critical Factors? Paper presented at the annual meeting of American Educational Research Association, 2006.

[17] Stenbhouse, L. An Introduction to Curriculum Research and Development. London: Heinemann, 1975.

[18] Wallace, W. J. Training Foreign Language Teachers: A Reflective Approach. Cambridge: CUP, 1991.

[19] Whitehead, J. Developing Personal Theories of Education. British Journal of In-Service Education, Vol. 9. No. 3, 1983.

注　解

1. 合作性教学（Cooperative Teaching）：本章讨论了欧美大学英语教师在博洛尼亚进程后怎样通过合作性教育手段促进英语教师的职业发展。合作性教学手段属于经验语言学习模式，其目的是培养英语教师通过合作学习从对方获取有用的信息，以增补自身在知识方面、教学方法等方面存在的不足。与学生一样，教师同样在个性、兴趣、动机、认识、经验方面存在着差异，这种差距为他们开展合作性的教学活动提供了基础，从而达到自我发展的目的。本章对合作途径提出了具体的方式方法，如教师与教师之间的合作、教师与学生之间的合作，这种互相支撑、互相学习的实践活动对教师心理上的满足、知识信息方面的更新都是有所裨益的。

2. 英语教师自我发展（ELT Teachers' Self-development）：教师发展应该贯穿英语教师从业的整个生涯，它是一个持续、不断发展提高的过程。在教学过程中，英语教师不断地对自己的教学行为进行调整、充实、增补、删减，注重自我反思、自我评估，使之成为更有效率的实践教师。反思是英语教师自我发展的核心，英语教师对自身行为进行不断地实践、思考、反思是教师职业发展的一种更高境界。本章将反思这一概念始终贯穿于当代欧美大学英语教师自身发展的三大模式中，即技艺模式、应用科学模式、反思模式。反思应用于英语教师的合作性教学活动无疑对教师的教学意识起到关键作用。教学观念的改变与更新将成为当代外语教师自身发展趋势的主流。

Chapter Five Reflective Teaching and English Teachers' Professional Development in Bologna Process

Since the second half of last century, great changes have taken place in ELT (English Language Teaching) and teacher education around the world. These changes symbolize "a shift from transmission, product-oriented theories to constructivist, process-oriented theories of learning, teaching, and teacher learning" (Crandall, 2000). In other words, in the teaching-learning binary structure, the attention and orientation of educators have been shifted from the outcomes to the process; the act of learning is regarded as an active process in which both teachers and learners generate new perspectives and novel ideas when referring back to and pondering on their past experiences. Therefore teachers start to undertake "observing their teaching acts, evaluating their outcomes, identifying problems, finding solutions, and trying them out to see once again what works and what does not" (Kumaravadivelu, 2001), after which the concept "reflection" is introduced and applied to tackle practical problems that conventional ways of teaching have failed to do.

As one of the significant reforms in education starting at the late 1990s, the Bologna process not only embraces and actively promotes the innovative educational concept of reflective teaching in Europe, but also in other countries all over the world. It is generally acknowledged among educators and scholars that reflection is the effective way for teachers to make changes and improvements in both their teaching practice and professional development and is one of the bases of enhancing ELT working efficiency. Recently, the concept of reflection has enjoyed wide popularity in the field of higher education and become an indispensable element of teachers' educational development (Richards, 2000). As a matter of fact, there are quite a lot of concepts closely related to reflective teaching in Western literary world, such as reflective thought, instructional decision-making, wisdom, critical thought, educational beliefs, views of self as a teacher, perceptions of teaching etc. (Cook, 1998). These concepts, or signs of reflective teaching, represent ELT teachers' approaches to advancing their teaching ability and professional development.

5.1 Understanding Reflective Teaching and Professional Development in ELT Education

In recent years, especially during the Bologna process in European and American colleges and universities, increasingly noticeable attention has been paid to the theories and practice of reflective teaching, and it has become of great significance that English language teachers constantly reflect upon their teaching experiences and activities as well their professional development, which becomes an effective way of improving the teachers' overall quality and the current situation of ELT education. Worldwide educators have proposed their understanding of this concept from diverse perspectives.

5.1.1 The Origin and Development of Reflective Teaching in Western Countries

The concept of reflection was firstly introduced by the prestigious American educator John Dewey in 1930s. Dewey pointed out that the current educational systems were fad-driven because educators studied how to do things instead of why the things were done (1933). In his book *How We Think: A Restatement of the Relation of Reflective Thinking to the Educational Process* (1933), Dewey criticizes habitual behaviors while calling for reflective or thoughtful conducts. He believes that teachers should be more rational than in the past and be capable of employing scientific teaching methods more skillfully and asserts that reflection in teaching can effectively improve teaching quality. According to him, education is not simply the repetition or imitation of the teaching techniques and methods of the past experiences, and good educators should learn to analyze the principles and techniques applied in the past and come up with new ones. He also asserts that the more teachers reflect on the past teaching experiences, the better their teaching quality will be. This is an interpretation of how reflective teaching works and how it is applied to teaching.

5 - 1 **John Dewey**

Besides, Dewey (1933) also classifies the indispensable prerequisite attitudes to reflective behaviors into three categories: open-mindedness, responsibility, and whole-heartedness. Open-mindedness refers to one's humble attitude that he or she is ready for accepting information from multiple sources, actively searches for, analyzes, and reflects on the possibilities, and embraces what was assumed as wrong. Responsibility is for the active self-examination of possible consequences of a certain action and the quick and effective responses. In other words, being responsible for their own behaviors means teachers should get rid of the existing impressions and conduct active investigations into the facts. Whole-heartedness means that the above mentioned two attitudes should be a lifelong guidance instead of a temporary principle for a teacher. These three guidelines play a significant role in guiding the revolution and development of education and should be viewed as the creed of teachers' teaching theories and practice. Dewey's theory of teaching practice has been generally accepted and adopted by teachers worldwide and remains pragmatic till now.

After Dewey, the term "reflective teaching" starts prevailing in education among Western countries and becomes one of the key topics of ELT educational innovation and development. Educators in US, UK, Canada and other countries of the world have illustrated the significance of "reflection" in teaching practice and teachers' education. Donald A. Schon (1983), the American thinker and educator, elaborates in details the concept of reflective behaviors and classifies them in chronological order. Schon holds that by combining the doubts and remaining questions with their own experiences, the practitioners, namely, the teachers, try to figure out ways to solve the questions through a series of reflective and studying activities, which is the most effective way to improve the practitioners' personal professional ability. Other educators such as Leo Bartlett (1997), Jack C. Richards and Charles Lockhart (1996), Kathleen. M. Bailey (2001), also interpret and argue about reflective teaching from both theoretical and practical perspectives.

5.1.2 Understanding Reflective Teaching

Regarding the definition of reflective teaching, scholars and educators have different yet unified interpretations. Cruickshank (1981) puts forward that reflective teaching means teachers reflect whatever has happened in class and consider to achieve a higher goal with different strategies and methods. Schon (1983) claims that reflective teaching refers to teachers' attempt to solve problems and erase doubts when they are confronted in the process of teaching through the employment of reflection. Richards (1992) unpacks reflective teaching by defining the term "reflection" from a macroscopic view, namely, reflection involves a series of actions including the recollection and examination of a past experience, based on which the evaluation and decision are made as well as the future plans and actions. Meanwhile, Richards also comments that Bartlett's definition of reflective teaching (1997) conforms to his understanding of the term "reflection", that is, in order to realize reflective teaching, teachers should go beyond the superficial reflection on the guiding teaching methods as well as those "how to" questions; instead, they should meditate on the "what" and "why" questions that are related to both the guiding and managing teaching methods, thus achieving a broader education goal. In other words, by constantly referring back to the past teaching experiences and considering what have been done in the classroom and why the teaching activities have been conducted in that way, teachers could gain a better cognition of their teaching behaviors and are empowered with more flexibility and autonomy in their teaching, which makes it possible to transform and perfect their teaching modes and even concepts.

As a matter of fact, Bailey, together with other co-authors (2001), classifies the various interpretations of reflective teaching into two categories in their book*Pursuing Professional Development*: *The Self as Source*. One interpretation is specific, focusing on teachers' self-reflective activities as individuals and emphasizing their behaviors and reflection before, during, and after class in their everyday teaching experiences. The other is broader, viewing reflection as an activity conducted not only in teachers' classroom teaching, but rather in the diversified social, political, and cultural con texts, such as the school, community, and even the entire society. Based on this categorization, Richards and Lockhart (1996) put forward their theory of reflective teaching, that is, teachers collect a wide range of different information during their teaching experiences to examine their teaching attitude, concepts, judgment, and teaching experience, which serves as the basis of further reflection on future teaching practice. While Richards and Lockhart's interpretation falls into the first category, Zeichner's explanation of reflective teaching is similar to the broader definition of the second one, namely, reflective teaching is teachers' recognition, examination, and speculation of their teaching ideas, experiences, attitude, knowledge, and values as well as the various limitations and opportunities in their working environments. Whatever it is defined as, reflective teaching is to bring the concepts of self-examination and self-reflection into teaching practice, motivating teachers to constantly deliberate on and perfect their teaching ideas and methods, advance their professional capability, and find their ways of professional development.

5.1.3 Major Features of Reflective Teaching

With "reflection" as the core concept and "teaching" as the basis, the development of reflective teaching proceeds with teachers as the guides and students both the subject and object of this revolution. Based on these key words and the diverse interpretations of reflective teaching, the features of reflective teaching are mainly exposed as follows:

(1) Reflective Teaching Connection with ELT teachers' Practice

Teachers' reflection on their teaching practice and the advancement of their teaching capacity are carried out and achieved in the teaching process. Therefore, apart from the theoretical guidance of the new concept, reflective teaching should also be evaluated and validated through teachers' teaching practice and activities.

(2) Reflective Teaching Ties with Students' Participation and Feedback

During reflective teaching, teachers dissect their own teaching practice, students' acceptance, and the teaching effects as the way of reflection. However, one of the ultimate goals of teachers' reflective teaching activities is to enhance their teaching quality so that students could learn more effectively. Therefore, as the major participants and subjects of feedback, students are actively involved in reflective teaching, and their acceptance and feedback mirror the effects and significance of their teachers' teaching practice. For example, according to Gibbs (2013), in recently years, some Ivy League universities have to adjust their curriculum by abandoning the generic writing courses offered by experts in communication as such efforts to improve students' writing are less effective than giving feedback on students' assignments and leading them to reflect on their own writing.

(3) Key of Reflective Teaching Autonomy and Initiative

Reflection is the essential way of enhancing teachers' professional attainments, and hence teachers' autonomy and initiative are manifested by their incessant examination of and reflection on their teaching styles, methods, and process from various perspectives. In addition, the issues that reflective teaching explores tend to be deemed by teachers as the most urgent, crucial and meaningful ones. In other words, the orientation of reflective teaching is teachers' own reflection on their own behaviors as well as the subsequent outcomes of the behaviors. As Cook (1998) remarks, distinguished from other thinkers, teachers are liable to be subjected to the so-called "ethical demand" when confronted with their objects, namely, their students, and teachers' responses to such a demand are the interpretation of the learner-centered teaching idea. Another factor is that teachers' impressions and emotions generated in their teaching experiences will also affect their reflections on their own teaching practice as well as the teaching outcomes.

(4) Reflective Teaching Association with Teachers' Professional Development

Teachers play multiple roles in the process of reflective teaching, ranging from the practitioner and the guide to the thinker and researcher. For teachers, in other words, teaching and research are integrated and reciprocal. In the process of reflective teaching, teachers observe the teaching practice of theirs and their peers, reflect on the teaching practice and students' feedback, and further perfect the new round of teaching practice, which helps improve teaching quality and effects. While consolidating, internalizing, and responding to the theoretical concepts, teachers could also establish and develop more refined teaching theories that can solve problems in future teaching practice, which will further advance their professional capability and achievements.

(5) Reflective Teaching Trend of Spiral Advancement

With teachers' constant observation, practice, reflection, and perfection, reflective teaching is circulating in the "teacher—students—teacher" teaching procedure, and its effects also follow the trend of spiral advancement.

5.2 Process and Strategies of Reflective Teaching in Bologna Process

Based on the various interpretations of reflective teaching, it can be deduced that what is involved in this practice is by no means a single incident or one-time effort. It requires a long, circulated process of practicing, recalling, unpacking, questioning, discussing, improving, and a new round of practice. In the field of English language teaching in Western countries in the Bologna process, a group of thinkers, educators, and scholars have studied the process of conducting reflective teaching and the strategies and methods of putting theories into practice.

5.2.1 Process of Reflective Teaching

Regarding the process, models, or frameworks of reflection in English language teaching, a wide range of theories have come into being and exert their influence in the literature. Silcock (1994) remarks that the analysis of the process of reflection has three components, namely, an ego-driven purpose, a restructuring capability and a transforming perspective. In other words, the act of reflection is conducted on purpose and with purpose; the past experience is remade by connecting new means to new ends; teachers are linked with their own presented and represented past experiences as well as their future possible practice. In their article "Beyond Method: The Rise of Reflective Teaching", Fat'hi and Behzadpour (2011) summarize a variety of dominant models of reflection and reflective teaching mentioned in the field of literature. Zeichner and Liston (1996) put forward five reflection phases rather than reflection content, which are rapid reflection, repair, review, research, and re-theorizing (cited in Fat'hi and Behzadpour, 2011). Stanley (1998) proposes a framework for teachers' reflectivity including five levels, namely, engaging with reflection, thinking reflectively, using reflection, sustaining reflection, and practicing reflection (cited in Fat'hi and Behzadpour, 2011).

Another work, Farrell's *Reflective Practice in Action*: 80 *Reflection Breaks for Busy Teachers* (2004), also comprises a list of models or frameworks of reflective teaching in English language teaching proposed by different scholars. Manen (1991) presents the model of a three-dimensional reflection: anticipatory reflection, active or interactive reflection, and recollective reflection (cited in Farrell, 2004). Day (1993), however, features reflection from his distinctive perspective as three levels: technical or rational level, conceptual level, and ethical, critical, or dialectical level (cited in Farrell, 2004). Pacheco (2005), citing Pickett (1996, p. 1), provides five components of critical reflection: identifying a problem, dealing with the problem by comparing it with other similar circumstances and taking into consideration its special context, evaluating and reevaluating the problem to obtain the solution, and "examining the intended and unintended consequences of an implemented solution and reevaluating the solution by determining whether the consequences are desirable or not" (cited in Fat'hi and Behzadpour, 2011, p. 8).

Based on the above discussed schools of processes and frameworks of reflective teaching, Farrell (2004) synthesizes different models of reflection and comes up with a more comprehensive model of reflection, which includes five stages. The first stage for teachers to start reflective teaching is to look back at and examine the teaching practice of themselves and their peers. There are quite a lot of effective ways to fulfil the task, including keeping teaching journals, collecting teaching portfolios, observing one another's classes, and discussing with peers the teaching practice. The second stage, after embarking on the reflective practice, is to collaborate to establish clear rules and regulations for all the activities involved in the process of observation, evaluation, and reflection, with the purpose that the teaching activities could be endowed with universality so as to be feasible for different participants. The third stage is to start planning the reflective practice. According to Farrell (2004), this stage of planning should include four time phases: individual time, activity time, development time, and reflection time. Individual time refers to the length of time each teacher allocates to the process of reflection. Although it varies from person to person, Farrell (2004) believes that every individual teacher, when collaborating with a group, is obliged to make it clear in the group how much time he or she can allot to the reflective practice. Another phase, activity time, means the amount of time devoted to each individual activity in the whole process of reflective practice. Development time, the third phase, represents the length of time each individual teacher allocates to the activities he or she carries out to master more sophisticated reflective practice. This time phase, accordingly, also differs from individual to individual. The last time phase, reflective time, signifies the amount of time teachers spend in group discussions. However, the word "reflective" here has double meanings: the whole process of the reflective practice and the act of reflection itself. In other words, reflective time refers to both the amount of time the group spends on the reflective practice and the time allocated to the act of reflection itself within the group. The fourth stage involves teachers' collaboration with one another in teaching, reflection and other related practice. To put it in another way, each teacher engaged in reflective practice should not only examine and reflect his or her own teaching practice as an individual, but also exchange ideas and updated information with one another to achieve the optimum effects of reflective teaching. The last stage is about the working atmosphere in the group work. The shift to reflective teaching practice, for most teachers, can be of paramount significance, and thus is likely to arouse uncertainty and anxiety. Individuals working in a group with an affective climate might receive reassurance and other positive signals, which will contribute to effective and successful group work in the process of reflective teaching practice.

5.2.2 Strategies of Reflective Teaching

Reflective teaching can be accomplished in various forms and ways in English language teaching practice. The methods and strategies of reflective teaching are involved in every aspect of the teaching practice and engage diversified subjects of teaching activities. Therefore, English language teachers are challenged to choose the most appropriate strategies and methods of reflective teaching in accordance with factors such as teaching context, content, and objects, namely, students, etc. The following are the most common and effective strategies that have been applied to reflective teaching practice conducted by college English teachers.

(1) Self-reflection of ELT Teachers

In each stage of the process of reflective teaching, the prerequisite and foundation of teachers' self-reflection are teaching activities. Therefore, the first step of teachers' self-reflection is to keep an objective and faithful record of their teaching practice and research into it afterwards. The forms of record vary, mainly classified into two categories: video/audio record and written record.

The video/audio record is the method of recording any moments and details throughout the teaching practice most faithfully. In the process of language teaching, the interaction between teachers and students are indispensable. In the activities carried out in a classroom, many detailed interaction between teachers and students are happening, and it is difficult for teachers to focus on every detail or remember it after the class. While recording the class activities, however, every detail is recorded, even including students' reaction to new questions and their feedback to the teaching effects, which provides the most faithful, first-hand material for teachers to reflect on after class. Teachers may listen to or watch the records repeatedly, find the problems that might exist in their teaching activities, and perfect the future teaching practice.

As another important method of teachers' self-reflection, written record is not only widely applied to foreign language teachers' reflective teaching activities, but also widely acknowledged in other disciplines in the education system. Richards (1992) classifies written records into three types: self-reports, autobiographies, and journal-writing. Self-reports refer to teachers' record of the teaching methods that have been employed in their teaching practice, which offers a way of evaluating teachers' teaching behaviors and effects after the perfection of their teaching methods through self-reflection. Autobiographies are the feedback records kept by both teachers and students after certain teaching activity. By analyzing the record, teachers are more liable to find the most and least effective teaching activities and reflect on them. Journal-writing is generally acknowledged as an effective and common tool in critical reflective teaching. Richards. J and Lockhart, C. (1996) recommend teachers to write the teaching journal, which records the context, process, effects of the teaching activities in class and the responses of both teachers and students to the class, to take down the problems or issues worth examining, and to note the positive points to gain more insights. Jarvis (1992) remarks that inferior journals simply list what happened in class or generally summarize the teaching process while the real remarkable and effective journals are favorable for solving problems, acquiring new teaching ideas and legitimizing the teaching practice. Through effective journal-writing, teachers can improve their ability to identify and analyze problems and to find the possible solutions.

While recording the teaching activities is to serve the purpose of the reflection on teaching practice, action research is another common way to theorize reflective teaching to enhance teachers' professional development. According to Bums (2011), action research is based on the fact that teachers are researchers. In other words, teachers adopt a self-reflective, critical, and systematic way to explore their own past teaching experiences, and with the results of their reflection, they try to tackle problematic situations in their new teaching practice from a new perspective in order to make changes and improvements in the upcoming teaching experiences. Kemmis and McTaggart (1988) propose that the typical action research involves four phases in a cycle of research, namely, planning, action, observation, and reflection (cited in Liu & Zhang, 2014). Action research is to summarize and theorize teachers' reflection on their own teaching practice, which in turn becomes the guidelines in teachers' reflective teaching activities, and is thereby an effective approach to teachers' professional development.

Throughout each phase of teaching practice, the self-reflection of teachers, one of the subjects of teaching activities, is a crucial way of reevaluating teachers' current concepts and behaviors. Teachers develop a direct and accurate understanding of such questions as what to teach and how to teach, which attributes to their improved ability to tackle problems and find solutions, and improve their professional capability.

(2) Collaborated Reflection of Teachers and Students

Apart from teachers' self-reflection, reflective teaching practice also requires the assist of other participants involved in teaching activities. Such collaborated reflection provides teachers with more resources, perspectives, and theoretical and practical knowledge. Therefore, the participation of students, the other subject of teaching practice, becomes indispensable. The most common methods of the collaborated reflection of teachers and students are presented as follows.

One type of collaboration is the interaction between teachers and students. In a foreign language class, the oral interaction between teachers and students through the use of the language is a significant way for students to develop a good command of the language. In teaching practice, teachers interact with students and thus observe their responses, including whether students are concentrated and engaged in class actively, whether students' analysis and answering questions are accurate, and whether students show enough interest in the class activities, etc. In this way, teachers gain a better understanding of students' language proficiency, capacity for acceptance as well as their initiative in study, which in turn will guide the next round of teaching practice.

Students' studying journal is students' feedback on the teaching activities. Students' regular journals may include the content of the teaching activities, their own performance, teachers' performance and its influence on them, the particular teaching content and methods that are easily and hardly accepted, etc. By doing this, students are endowed with the autonomy and initiative as the subject of teaching practice and are encouraged to make their voices heard in finding and solving problems related to study. From students' perspectives, teachers are able to develop a more comprehensive understanding of their own teaching behaviors, which guarantees a more effective evaluation of and reflection on their teaching practice. In addition, teachers might also exchange their teaching journals with students' studying journals and find the overlap and discrepancy to achieve more remarkable improvements in teaching.

Students' evaluation on teaching is another way of collaborative reflection. A variety of approaches can be adopted by students to observe, evaluate, and supervise teachers' teaching activities to magnify the reflective teaching effects. The most common evaluation methods include students' forums organized by the teaching management administrators of the college, questionnaires for students, online evaluation, etc. Teachers acquire students' direct feedback on their teaching practice and discover strengths and weaknesses of their teaching activities, thereby evaluating and adjusting their teaching strategies and improving their teaching capability.

(3) Peer Reflection

As in any other fields, teachers are in constant need of the teamwork with their peers, in either teaching or research practice. Only by reflecting on their own and absorbing others' teaching concepts, strategies, and specific methods can teachers enhance their professional capability. A large number of ways of collaborative reflection among peer teachers have been employed, among which the following three are considered common and effective.

Observation and communication of one another's teaching practice is one of the most common ways of teachers' collaborative reflection. Usually the observing and communicating activities are carried out among teachers offering the same class or using the same textbooks. Teachers observing their peers' classroom activities pay special attention to how other teachers control the class, allocate teaching content, organize class activities, adopting teaching methods, and dealing with various events occurring in the classroom, etc., and record which aspects in this class are successful and what might need improving. These series of activities are then followed by the exchanges of both parties' ideas and the cooperation in coming up with positive plans for further amelioration. Teachers obtain the opportunities to observe, feel, and learn distinctive teaching styles and ideas from their peers, and reflect on one another's teaching practice critically, which broadens teachers' horizon in reflective teaching practice and ensures the achievement of the goal of mutual development.

Another way is collaborative teaching journal. Apart from teachers' own teaching journal and students' studying journal, as Richards (1992) mentions, teachers' collaborative teaching journal is another effective way of enhancing reflective teaching. Collaborative teaching journal is teachers' record of their own teaching experiences as part of the teamwork. Teachers in the same group meet regularly, share each other's teaching journal, and discuss their own experience in teaching and keeping journals. Moreover, the group can also compile the members' teaching journals, feedback on each other's journal, and the results of group discussion and reflection to explore the effects of the interactions among teachers. Richards (1992) summarizes the multifold benefits brought by collaborative journal-keeping to the professional development of second language teachers. He notes that collaborative journal-keeping raises teachers' awareness of the importance of classroom processes and the constant reflection on them; it serves as a reservoir of various teaching ideas and practice that teachers can learn and share; it also provides role models, support, and encouragement in a more acceptable way.

A third choice of ways peer reflection is teaching evaluation. The forms of teaching evaluation can be various, including teachers' self-evaluation, students' evaluation of teachers' performance, peer evaluation among teachers, as are mentioned above, and also the evaluation given by the educational administrators and supervisors of the college. While receiving the evaluation given by their peers, teachers acquire valuable ideas and suggestions from different perspectives, which help them to further reflect on their own teaching behaviors. The college's evaluation team composed of experienced teachers and educational experts offers guidance and advice to teachers after observing their teaching activities, which contributes to the promotion of teachers' teaching ability and professional capacity.

Johnson County Community College (JCCC for short), the largest undergraduate institution of higher education in the state of Kansas, the United States, is a good example of carrying out reflective teaching, especially in its English teaching programs. In the US, community colleges are one kind of common higher educational institutions. Also entitled two-year colleges, community colleges offer courses to students and grant diplomas and associate's degrees. After graduation, students can transfer to a four-year college or university for two to three years to complete a bachelor's degree. The advantages of a community college include lower tuition fees, smaller-scale classes, and rich teaching resources, which facilitate students, especially language learners, with better opportunities to intensively enhance their language proficiency.

5 - 2 **Johnson County Community College**

5 - 3 **Johnson County Community College**

For instance, professional development events are organized at JCCC a week before each new semester for staff members to meet and discuss each other's teaching experiences. These events range from series of training for the online teaching systems to table discussions. The tables are of different topics on which experts and experienced teachers are invited to give informal presentations to other participants at the table. The topics include sharing of best teaching practices, building outside-the-classroom relationship with students, handling difficult students, library resources, so on and so forth. All the staff members are encouraged to visit and change tables after each session, reflecting on their own personal teaching experiences and exchanging ideas with one another to achieve mutual improvements. Besides that, teaching evaluations, with detailed and insightful questions on the evaluation forms, are also given by both the students and peers as the feedback on teachers' teaching activities from various perspectives during each semester, which help teachers develop a better understanding of their teaching behaviors and effects. Moreover, the English department at JCCC runs a blog which is regularly updated with the ongoing news, sharing of syllabi and other teaching sources, calling for papers and proposals for teaching conventions held both on the campus and in other colleges or universities in the nearby cities. In addition, teaching conferences are also held on the campus with prestigious keynote speakers and other presenters as well as sessions for teachers to share, evaluate, and perfect each other's teaching practice. Such reflective activities have been greatly motivating the amelioration of both teachers' teaching capability and their professional development at JCCC.

5.3 Significance of Reflective Teaching for ELT Teachers' Professional Development in Bologna Process

With the Bologna process proceeding, foreign languages, especially English, play a significant role in the globalization of knowledge and culture as a crucial tool of communication in Europe and other countries around the world. English teachers should equip themselves with substantial professional knowledge, proficiency in teaching and research, moral attainments, and the potential for sustainable development. English teachers cannot grow and develop without the accumulation of everyday teaching experiences, and only with the constant reflection on their teaching practice can teachers be qualified to gain new and more mature experience and be further motivated to achieve the improvements of integrated capability. In other words, reflective teaching is of momentous theoretical and realistic significance for English teachers' professional development.

5.3.1 Significance of Reflective Teaching for Teachers' Accumulation of Professional Knowledge

Foreign language teachers' professional knowledge can be a broad concept, ranging from the structure, function, practice, and the inherent logic of the language itself to the in-depth interpretation and study of related professional theories, such as educational theories, educational psychology, linguistics, etc. In addition, in foreign language teaching activities, the accumulated empirical and theoretical knowledge functions as guidance in teachers' professional development, and is thus one fundamental component of foreign language teachers' professional knowledge.

The British thinker, Polyni (1993), proposes that human knowledge is composed of two parts: explicit knowledge and tacit knowledge. The explicit knowledge, self-evidently, refers to the knowledge that people possess and use to communicate accurately. On the contrary, the tacit knowledge is what cannot or hardly be conveyed with verbal or written language, or signs, and is characterized as illogical, non-communal, and circumstantial. According to Polyni, though existing in every domain of the society and every level of human knowledge, tacit knowledge can be neither formalized nor acquired by direct teaching of others; instead, it can only be established and acquired by oneself in a specific field, through the practical experiences of completing tasks, constant reflection, and summary, and thus can only be conveyed by the practitioner's own language (cited in Jin, 2006). Humans' pursuit and acquisition of knowledge is incessant, their command of knowledge forever changing; thereby, humans should enrich their tacit knowledge by ceaseless accumulation and validate the knowledge through constant critical reflection.

Through personal experiencing, accumulating, and practicing, foreign language teachers have a command of rich tacit knowledge, which needs activating and evaluating through continuous practice and thus gets its validity and significance verified. Reflective teaching is an important way for foreign language teachers to accumulate and verify the tacit knowledge and practical knowledge. At the beginning of the reflective teaching, teachers determine the teaching goals, content, methods, and solutions to problems through reflection; during the reflective teaching practice, teachers integrate professional theoretical knowledge with practical knowledge to guide their teaching practice and observe the effects; after the teaching practice, teachers summarize and reflect on the teaching activities, hence adjusting their knowledge system and teaching methods. In addition, throughout the practice of reflective teaching, foreign language teachers critically summarize and reflectively evaluate their performance, which helps integrate the results of reflection with their own professional knowledge, and thus achieve the reconstruction and enrichment of their professional knowledge. Such practice enables teachers to not only accumulate the knowledge gained from actions, but also reflect on the tacit knowledge obtained subconsciously and continue to create new knowledge. In this process of constant questioning, reflection, adjustment and accumulation, the professional knowledge of foreign language teachers in both theory and practice has been continuously developed and substantiated, laying a solid knowledge foundation for their professional development.

5.3.2 Significance of Reflective Teaching for Teachers' Teaching Proficiency

Teacher's major responsibility is to impart knowledge and learning ability to students through teaching activities. For foreign language teachers, reflective teaching practice is more than a specific method of making new teaching plans, gaining more experiences in future teaching practice or more knowledge about how to teach, but a guideline or a concept that keeps inspiring them to challenge what they have been accustomed to. It contributes to teachers' development of the habit of exploring and the ability to integrate new findings into future theoretical and practical work, and their motivation for establishing new teaching ideas and methods. In other words, reflective teaching transforms foreign language teachers from the empirical and expert type into the reflective type, which impels teachers to constantly improve their teaching proficiency. It is embodied in three aspects.

(1) Reflective Teaching Adjustment Roles

In traditional language teaching practice, teachers played a leading role as knowledge transmitters. However, according to Wang (2000), foreign language teachers should play nine different roles according to different teaching situations: controller, assessor, organizer, prompter, participant, resource-provider, facilitator, guide and researcher (cited in Liu & Zhang, 2014). Through reflection, both teachers and students adjust and re-adjust their roles in the teaching-learning practice. Teachers' roles of guide, facilitator, and participant guarantee students' position to be another subject in the teaching activities. In other words, in reflective teaching practice, students enjoy the same, equal status with their teachers. Instead of passively receiving knowledge, students begin to actively engage themselves in the teaching activities and give their feedback on teachers' performance, which contributes to more productive teaching and learning effects.

(2) Reflective Teaching Transformation

Gradually formed in the process of teaching experiences, teachers' teaching concepts, together with their teaching habits, styles, and methods, are influenced by their learning experiences, knowledge structure as well as teaching experiences. These concepts, in turn, affect teachers' performance in teaching practice. In the process of reflective teaching, however, teachers gradually get more accustomed to and more skillful in rationally summarizing, evaluating, and improving every single aspect of their teaching activities, including teaching plans, ideas, strategies, methods, etc. The constant questioning and assessment of their teaching performance and the reflection on it inspire teachers to adjust and improve their teaching plans and activities, which magnifies the teaching effects and ameliorates teachers' teaching proficiency.

(3) Reflective Teaching Integration Theory with Practice

Any theory needs verifying by being put into practice and guiding the practice. Educational theories are originated from abundant teaching practice. In their daily teaching activities, foreign language teachers, based on their teaching theories, reflect on anything involved in the classroom teaching: concepts, targets, content, facilities, methods, styles, etc. They proceed to evaluate their own performance, issues exposed, and students' responses. Through reflection, teachers develop a new understanding of educational theoretical and practical knowledge, which guides the new cycle of teaching activities. In other words, the goal of reflective teaching is to achieve more reasonable teaching practice. On the basis of the current research achievements, foreign language teachers reflect on their teaching activities and come up with their own updated theories, which are the embodiment of the integration of theory and practice. In a word, through reflective teaching, teachers constantly perfect their ability to integrate theory and practice, thus laying a solid foundation for their research proficiency and professional development.

5.3.3 Significance of Reflective Teaching for Teachers' Research Proficiency

In the Bologna process in recent years, the emergence and development of reflective teaching represent the epistemological and methodological turn in education in the western world, namely, the shift from the traditional "scientific" paradigm to the "humanistic" paradigm. The steering system draws people's attention to the knowledge system and professional skills formed in teachers' professional teaching activities. The "knowledge" and "skills" mentioned here refer to the individual theoretical and practical knowledge. In the reflective teaching activities, on the basis of the educational teaching theories and experiences of the teachers and their peers, and with the teaching activities as the content of reflection, foreign language teachers analyze and evaluate their own teaching performance, process, psychology, effects, and students' feedback, and thus achieve the virtuous cycle of finding out problems, solving problems, and perfecting teaching practice. The results of reflection, in turn, serve as the guidance for the new cycle of teaching activities, which refine teachers' teaching concepts and enrich their theoretical and practical knowledge. Such ever updated understandings gradually become the foundation of the teachers' own teaching theories, which further guide the new round of teaching practice.

In addition, reflective teaching also motivates teachers to meticulously observe and reflect on the complex and diverse teaching activities and encourages students to develop strong autonomy and initiative during the learning process, to collaboratively uncover the problems in teaching and learning activities and come up with effective solutions. At the same time, through the incessant study of teaching theories and the interaction and discussion with their peers after the demonstration of each other's classes, teachers can enrich and refine their own educational theories, which will be more qualified to guide new teaching practice. The teachers' creativity and logic get developed in this process, thereby facilitating the advancement of their research capability.

5.3.4 Significance of Reflective Teaching for Teachers' Professional Moral Attainments

As educators, foreign language teachers undertake the responsibility of fostering students' ability to acquire knowledge, subjectivity, and moral attainments, and play a momentously significant role in students' learning and accumulation of knowledge as well as the cultivation of their personality. In the teaching activities, teachers should be responsible for their students, their own teaching performance, and their own professional development. Therefore, teachers' professional development is inseparable from the cultivation of their professional moral attainments.

In the reflective teaching practice, from any of the perspectives of the content of reflection, procedure of reflection, or the specific methods, the key issues of foreign language teachers' reflection are always facing the problems in their own teaching practice, analyzing and reflecting on the problems objectively and comprehensively, and innovating for new practice. In other words, the process of reflective teaching is one during which teachers accept their past teaching behaviors, reflect on them, and get ready for the changes in future teaching activities. The teachers may transform themselves through reflection, but only when they take the initiative to accept their past and take the responsibility for the outcomes can they achieve real effective improvements. Therefore, in the process of reflective teaching, teachers have the courage to assume full responsibility for their behaviors and performance in various stages of their teaching activities, reflect on the past teaching experiences continuously, actively collaborate with their students and colleagues, and embrace the feedback on their teaching behaviors and outcomes. This process helps the teachers discover the problems exposed in their teaching practice, explore the reasons and solutions, and verify the solutions in future teaching activities. In this way, teachers pursue more reasonable teaching practice so as to effectively ameliorate their teaching quality and effects.

5.3.5 Significance of Reflective Teaching for Teachers' Sustainable Development

Teachers' professional development is not what can be achieved all at once. When developing their professional quality, foreign language teachers need, in addition to the long-term, persistent accumulation and practice, a strong and incessant driving force, which can assist them in exploring and giving scope to their potential of professional development and thus enable them to achieve the sustainable development. Reflective teaching, undoubtedly, plays a key role in this process.

In the process of reflective teaching, teachers are emboldened to rethink their past teaching behaviors, to redefine their roles and functions in the teaching activities, to obtain the feedback from the interaction with their peers and students, and to make constant adjustments under the given circumstances. That means the challenge and surpass of the past teaching concepts and behaviors of the teachers as the subject of the teaching activities, and it represents the reconstruction of teachers' theoretical and practical knowledge in teaching, the re-planning for the future teaching concepts and behaviors, and the further perfection of their professional quality. Reflective teaching provides a new direction of scientific research for foreign language teachers. The reflective teaching, as a matter of fact, is the process in which the teachers put into practice their theoretical knowledge and teaching experience, reflect on the teaching process, and enrich and modify their theoretical and practical knowledge in teaching. This is the process of foreign language teachers' conduct of scientific research and their advancement of professional capability. The professional development should be a continuous, sustainable, and spiral trend. Adhering to the concept of reflective teaching, teachers will gain the awareness of achieving remarkable professional development and the huge potential for such development. The reflective concept in foreign language teaching functions as a positive motivation for the improvement of teachers' theoretical quality. It has opened up a new way to refine the teachers' knowledge system and provided a new mentality for teachers to magnify their teaching quality, which will undoubtedly broaden the field of their professional development and serve as an immense impetus for their sustainable development.

5.4 ELT Challenge and Dilemma in Developing Reflective Teaching

The purpose of language teaching, especially English language, in colleges and universities of both European countries and other countries around the world, is to cultivate students' comprehensive ability to employ the language to achieve the effective verbal and written communication in social contact, to enhance their capability of independent learning, and to foster their cultural quality. Therefore, college English teachers and educators must innovate for new teaching concepts and ideas, applying more effective teaching strategies and methods to English language teaching activities. With teachers as the guide and students the subjects, reflective teaching intends to give full scope to teachers' potential and creativity in teaching and professional development and to cultivate students' learning autonomy and initiative.

In recently years, however, as the concept of reflective teaching has been generally discussed by educators worldwide, no agreement has ever reached on the definition and aims of reflective teaching, the content on which teachers should reflect, the process of carrying out reflective teaching activities, or the roles of both teachers and students in reflective teaching. Consequently, devising and developing reflective teaching programs becomes quite a challenging task, which requires not only the designation of new teaching practice, but the consideration of many essential factors involved in this innovative educational concept, such as the difficulties in conveying the idea and purpose of reflective teaching to all those involved (including teachers, students, administrators, etc.), the reconciliation with conventional teaching as well as with the social and institutional restrictions that are more inclined to support the conventional, etc. (Calderhead, 1993). Though reflective teaching has exhibited its unparalleled advantages as educational innovation in college English teaching activities and made considerable positive accomplishments, a number of difficulties and dilemmas as follows reoccur and are worth noticing among English teachers and educators.

5.4.1 How to Balance Different Focuses of Reflective Teaching

In his "Dilemmas in Developing Reflective Teaching," Calderhead (1993) makes a list of eight different dilemmas involved in reflective teaching when educators attempt to devise and design reflective teaching programs, and the firstly mentioned one is how to conceptualize the substance of reflective teaching programs and how to balance the focuses involved in teachers' application of reflective teaching theories. In other words, in the process of teachers' accepting and employing reflective concepts, due to the general lack of an agreed definition of this concept and the cognition of the required knowledge, skills, and even attitudes that might be involved in reflective teaching, it is especially difficult for teachers to balance the time and energy that are supposed to be devoted to different focuses of reflective teaching. What should be the major focus of teachers' self-training for reflective teaching concepts and practice? Apparently, it is possible that the development of one of the focuses might be at the cost of the others. Therefore, how to acquire a scientific understanding of the concept of reflective teaching, the strategies, and skills to put the concept into practice and achieve optimum effects, and the rational attitude with which teachers will be able to carry out reflective teaching activities as a constructive practice becomes a crucial matter in English teachers' awareness and development of reflective teaching.

Another issue related to English teachers' self-training of reflective teaching is the compatibility and balance of instruction and autonomy for teachers. On the one hand, reflective teaching requires a whole new set of knowledge, skills, and attitudes that are predefined, and teachers need to learn from the more experienced in order to develop a new one. On the one hand, as is discussed in the previous sections, observing classes in order to learn from and discuss with peers is one effective method in reflective teaching. On the other hand, however, with the open and ever-developing trend of reflective teaching, teachers are encouraged and constantly motivated to develop autonomy in designing their own reflective teaching procedure and strategies and take responsibility for their own professional development. Therefore, how to achieve the compatibility between conforming to the learnt knowledge and exercising teachers' autonomy is a challenge in reflective teaching.

5.4.2 How to Keep Balance in the Inner Mechanism of Reflective Teaching Process and Content

Given the wide range of various opinions on the process and content of reflective teaching practice, as well as the complicated components of various reflective teaching processes and objects contended by different educators and scholars, it becomes all the more challenging for teachers to keep the balance in the inner mechanism of reflective teaching process and content, including mainly the following four aspects.

(1) Balance of Different Stages of Reflective Teaching Process

Since English teaching activities are mainly carried out in the classroom, teachers involved in reflective teaching tend to place more importance on the after-class stage, among the three stages of pre-class, in-class, and after-class of the teaching process. Teachers reflect on the whole teaching process, their own teaching behaviors, students' performance, and the teaching effects. Students, on the other side, are encouraged to evaluate their learning experience, which is usually accomplished when completing their task of learning in class. Nevertheless, as to the reflection before and during the teaching and learning practice, both teachers and students fail to pay enough attention. As a matter of fact, the reflection before teaching focuses on the ideas, design, content, and methods of the teaching-learning practice; the reflection during teaching is on the generation of dynamic events in the classroom; and the reflection after teaching attaches more importance to the teaching effects as well as its consistency with the pre-class design. The reflection on the three stages of teaching is closely interrelated, constituting the basic means of guiding the teaching practice. Keeping the balance among the stages is challenging but crucial.

In addition, another common problem in reflective teaching is, at the stage of pre-teaching practice, teachers are liable to set more ambitious target than what they may actually be able to achieve (Calderhead, 1993). It is a tough task for teachers to be aware of their own values and beliefs, their ability to evaluate their own teaching practice, as well as the social and educational context of their teaching activities. Only by taking into consideration all these factors and with considerable teaching experiences can teachers reasonably expect what aim is possible to achieve and what ways are feasible to carry out in a long term, which is a hard question for teachers to consider and tackle.

(2) Balance of Teachers' Reflection and Students' Reflection

Influenced by the conventional teaching concept, in reflective teaching activities, teachers are inclined to take the leading role while neglecting the students' position as subjects as well as the fact that the learning process is the one during which students construct their own knowledge structure. Therefore, reflection should be made by both teachers and students without the special emphasis on either one, especially on teachers. As the matter of fact, in the reflective teaching process of college English, more attention should be given to the cultivation of students' habit of reflecting on their own learning behaviors. Learning English is a practical process of cognition, so whether students can learn English well depends largely on their learning behaviors, attitudes, and habits.

5 - 4 **Oxford Brookes University**

5 – 5 **Harvard University**

For example, when working as a "study skills counsellor" as Oxford Polytechnic (now called Oxford Brookes University), Gibbs (2013) noticed that the biggest difference between effective students and bewildered students is that the former know to be reflective and ready for changes and adjustments in their study plans, tasks, and methods. Such so-called effective "study skills" enable students to be aware of what they are doing, what changes they need to make, the different possibilities they have, and the adjustments they need to make to receive better learning effects. On the contrary, however, a research at Harvard University showed that some bright students sometimes failed to have a proper understanding of what learning means and what its purpose is. Consequently, these students tend to memorize the right answers of some problems for a test, which is called "quantitative accretion of discrete rightness" (Gibbs). Such learning habits are the outcomes of an unreflective learning process, and thus cause their failure of being successful students in one of the world's best universities. In a word, only with good learning habits cultivated through reflection can students develop the ability to learn and evaluate, and to creatively analyze and solve problems on their own. Teachers, on the other hand, should attach importance to the cultivation of students' reflective learning ability and their feedback on teaching activities in order to optimize the quality and effects of the reflective teaching practice.

(3) Balance of Teaching Content and Context in Reflective Teaching

In the process of college English reflective teaching, some teachers tend to confine the content of teaching within the scope of vocabulary, grammar, and language points while neglecting to uncover the association between the teaching materials and students' actual life as well as the social and cultural context. Consequently, students are trapped in the wrong impression that there is no direct link between the content and context, thus losing interest in learning and reflecting. How to direct education to the return to "life" and integrate teaching content with the social and cultural context in which teachers and students are living in so that students are more willing to learn and think should be one of the goals of reflective teaching. It is urgent, thereby, for teachers to review their teaching concepts, unearth more and richer course resources to meet the needs of students' intellectual, emotional, and psychological development, and help students to construct their knowledge structure in a vivid and familiar context, thus achieving the goal of mutual development of both teachers and students.

5.4.3 How to Solve the Conflicts with Traditional Teaching Values

Innovation means challenge to the traditional. Naturally, the values embodied in reflective teaching about teaching practice and about teachers' professional development, to some extent, expose as a challenge to the traditional teaching values and are inevitably in conflict with the traditional. For instance, reflective teaching promotes the concept that teachers invest time to analyze their past teaching experiences and the educational worth of such practice is often at odds with the traditional values of more immediate, reflective action (Calderhead, 1993), which casts doubt on the concept of reflective teaching and makes the process full of twists and turns. In addition, before teachers enter the profession of teaching, they, as students, have received the education with more traditional values and concepts, and have been endowed with expectations which are different from those of reflective teaching. However, one of the major thrusts of reflective teaching is to examine any given practice critically before accepting it, which signifies that the new teachers should reassess what they have learnt and accepted when they were students from a critical perspective. The reconciliation between the conflicting values may become an impediment to the new teachers when they come into the profession with the course of innovative reflective teaching. Therefore, how to keep balance between the two sets of values of the traditional and the innovative and how to reach the reconciliation may present a constant difficulty for teachers involved in reflective teaching.

Calderhead (1993) compares traditional teacher educators who train and educate new generation of teachers to gatekeepers, whose function is to assess the new teachers' performance to ensure that only those who are competent in and committed to their teaching career are qualified to enter the profession. However, reflective teaching requires teachers to be critical to the teaching practice of both themselves and their peers, to be concerned about different stages of teaching practice, and to be open-minded to accept diversified teaching ideas and strategies. The criteria for teachers' qualifications, thereby, are different, including not only the competence in the teachers' teaching behaviors, but also that in their awareness of having critical thinking and being open to any possibility. Consequently, teachers engaged in reflective teaching should be ready to confront the traditional teaching concepts and to embrace the changes and adjustments they will make during the transition from tradition to innovation.

5.4.4 How to Reconcile the Notion of the Individual and the Collective

As is discussed above, teachers start to learn how to teach in different ways, based on their own past experiences even when they were students, and they may have different ideas and methods in teaching formed in their own particular context and background. And reflective teaching demands that teachers should be critical to the established teaching values and notions, open to embrace different possibilities in teaching, and give full scope to their individual potential in teaching practice. Therefore, individualism in reflective teaching should be highly promoted to enrich the ideas, beliefs, and specific strategies of the new teaching notion, which may make it all the more difficult to handle, but in turn will help facilitate teachers' professional development (Calderhead, 1993).

Some educators, however, suggest that reflective teaching practice requires a supportive environment in which it is fostered and developed (Zeichner & Liston, 1987). In other words, reflection is the process of individual's internal activities, but it is also like a social, public activity, which demands a platform for teachers to experience and discuss together. Therefore, in the process of reflective teaching, college English teachers should not be confined to the concept of "self", but actively engage themselves in the collaborative reflecting work in a group. With the shared resources, teachers are endowed with more opportunities to learn from and evaluate each other's teaching practice, find the gap in both concepts and methods, and further advance one another's professional development. These two notions raise the question of whether reflective teaching should set the aim of more related to the display of teachers' individual talents or the collective effort of teachers as a group. Therefore, how to reconcile the notions of individualism and collectivism poses another repeated question to reflective teaching on the way to achieving the optimum teaching effects and teachers' professional development.

In a nutshell, given to the difficulties and dilemmas existing in reflective teaching in Bologna process, the process of establishing and developing reflective teaching concepts and programs has been and will be one full of challenges. Nevertheless, with teachers taking into consideration those factors and actively seeking for countermeasures, reflective teaching is still a notion with vitality and potential in English language teaching. It will display its unsurpassed advantages in innovating college English teaching and advancing teachers' professional capability and development in colleges and universities of the Western countries and the rest of the world.

Bibliography

[1] Bailey, K. M. et al. Pursuing Professional Development: The Self as Source [M]. Boston: Heinle & Heinle, 2001.

[2] Bums, A. Doing Action Research in English Language Teaching: A Guide for Practitioners [M]. Beijing: Foreign Language Teaching and Research Press, 2011.

[3] Calderhead, J. Dilemmas in Developing Reflective Teaching [J]. Reflective Teaching and Teacher Education, 1993 (20).

[4] Cook, P. F. Teacher Reflection in Learner-centered Education [M].

Reform Forum: Journal for Educational Reform in Namibia, 1998.

[5] Crandall, J. A. Language Teacher Education [J]. Annual Review of Applied Linguistics, 2000 (20).

[6] Cruickshank, D. R., and Applegate, J. H. Reflective Teaching as a Strategy for Teacher Growth [M]. Alexandria: Educational Leadership, 1981.

[7] Dewey, J. How to Think: A Restatement of the Relation of Reflective Thinking to the Educative Process [M]. Boston: D. C. Heath, 1933.

[8] Farrell, T. Reflective Practice in Action: 80 Reflection Breaks for Busy Teachers [M]. California: Corwin Press, 2004.

[9] Fat'hi, J., and Behzadpour, F. Beyond Method: The Rise of Reflective Teaching [J]. International Journal of English Linguistics, 2011 (1).

[10] Gibbs, G. Teaching Intelligence: Self-reflective Improvement [N]. Times Higher Education, 2013.

[11] Jarvis, J. Using Diaries for Teacher Reflection in Service Courses [J]. ELT Journal, 1992 (46).

[12] Kumaravadivelu, B. Toward a Postmethod Pedagogy [J]. TESOL Quarterly, 2001 (35).

[13] Liu, L., and Zhang, Y. Enhancing Teachers' Professional Development Through Reflective Teaching [J]. Theory and Practice in Language Studies, 2014 (4).

[14] Richards, J. C. Beyond Training [M]. Cambridge: Cambridge University Press, 2000.

[15] Richards, J. C., and Lockhart, C. Reflective Teaching in Second Language Classrooms [M]. London: Cambridge University Press, 1996.

[16] Schon, D. A. The Reflective Practitioner: How Professionals Think in Action [M]. New York: Basic Book, 1983.

[17] Silcock, P. The Process of Reflective Teaching [J]. British Journal of Educational Studies, 1994 (42).

[18] Zeichner, K., and Liston, D. P. Reflective Teaching: An Introduction [M]. Mahwah, N. J.: L. Erlbaum Associates, 1996.

[19] 熊川武：《反思性教学》，上海：华东师范大学出版社 1999 年版。

注　解

1. 反思性教学（Reflective Teaching）：反思性教学被国内外教育界认为是促进教师教育发展的重要途径。反思性教学与教师的教学实践紧密相关，重新定位教师与学生在教学活动中的角色，着重培养和发挥二者作为教学活动主体的主观能动性。在反思性教学过程中，教师通过观察、思考、改变并在实践中进行进一步的检验和修正，从而改进自己的教学行为，提升教学质量。同时，在巩固、内化并反馈理论概念的过程中，又可以建立和发展能够解决教学实践问题的教学理论，从而提升教师自身的职业能力和专业素养。因此反思性教学的导向是源于教师自身的思考，并通过“教师—学生—教师”这一教学实践流程实现螺旋上升的发展趋势，成为教师实现可持续专业发展的必要途径。

2. 同级反思（Peer Reflection）：同级反思是指在大学英语的反思性教学过程中，教师之间开展的相互反思性活动。教师通过课堂观摩与讨论、合作教学日记、教学评估等方式对彼此的教学活动进行观察、学习、讨论，反思自身与他人的教学理念、策略、方法等，以实现提高专业水平、推动职业发展的共同目标。

3. 显性知识和隐性知识（Explicit Knowledge and Tacit Knowledge）：显性知识和隐性知识的概念是由英国科学家、哲学家波兰尼于1933年提出的。显性知识又称为“明确知识”“明言知识”或“言名知识”等，指的是用书面文字、图标以及数学公式等方式表示的知识。隐性知识又称为“缄默知识”“默会知识”“默然知识”等，指的是尚未被言语或者其他形式所表述的知识。例如，人们在做某事的行动中所拥有的知识便属于隐性知识。

Chapter Six Ecology of Education and ELT Teachers' Development in Bologna Process

Ecology is not a new discipline. Firstly proposed in the 19th century, it is a study on the interaction between organisms and the environment which they are living in. Within a century, it has been developed into an ideological system. At the beginning of the 20th century, the ideas, principles, and methods of ecology are widely applied to sociology and other areas, thus the ecology of education coming into being. Integrated with the ideas and theories of ecology such as information, system, and control, the ecology of education focuses on a wide range of phenomena in education as well as the causes, studies the basic rules of education, and reveals the orientation and trend of educational development (Cao, 2011). Gradually, it covers various aspects of education, including the mutual influence of the education and the natural and social environment on each other, as well as the relationship between individuals and groups composing the whole ecological system of education, educational activities, and the environment where the activities take place, thereby demonstrating the rules and principles of the ecological system of education (Leather, 2003). With strong vitality, the ecology of education has been a teaching concept and strategy widely adopted by an increasing number of educators and teachers so far.

Since an ideal ecological learning environment is crucial to language learning, the modern information technologies of computers and internet have been proposed and applied by many educators and integrated with students and the language learning process to create a harmonious ecological learning environment. When computers and individuals are considered as integration in the human-computer society, computers and internet are no longer objects excluded from this ecological system, but an indispensable chain in this system (Chen, 2005). With a long-term plan, the goal of Bologna process is to set up a common higher education system in Europe. Sweden, for instance, has a lifelong education mode and is one of the participants of the Bologna process, dedicating to improving the competitive ability of teachers' education with the implement of the integrated European higher education system. Information technology has created new opportunities in higher education in Swedish universities. With a rising number of exchanged students from other European countries, the development of the international network learning is all the more popular, gradually forming a worldwide network learning system and promoting other European countries to follow suit. In other words, in the Bologna process, the rising and development of the internet education and teachers' education are the reflection of the ideas of an ecological learning environment where the learning individuals (namely, students) and the computers as well as internet are integrated and create profound learning and teaching effects.

6.1 Current Study of Ecology of Education in ELT

The origin of the study on the ecology of education can be dated back to 1940s when Barker and Wright from University of Kansas in the United States started a research center of ecology on human behavior, namely, Midwest Psychological Field Station (Fan, 1995). Their research shows that the principles and approaches of ecology can be applied to the study of humans and human society. In 1966, the concept of "ecology of higher education" was proposed by the American educator, Ashby, which started the research on higher education based on the science of ecology (cited in Fan, 1995). In 1970s, more efforts were made to study ecology of human development and the relationship between individual behavior and environment in the context of schools.

In 1976, Lawrence Cremin proposed the concept of "ecology of education" for the first time, which symbolizes that ecology has been assimilated into education as well as its branches, becoming a new area of research. According to Cremin (1976), the ecology of education adopts the theories of applied ecology, especially those on ecological systems, ecological balances, etc., to study various phenomena in education and their reasons, uncover the rules and principles of educational development, and disclose its future developing trend. In 1977, the British scholar Eggleston published a book in which the resources of ecology of education in schools were studied. Later on in 1978, Cremin gave a speech on the revolution in ecology of education, in which his ideas of the ecology of education were further illustrated. According to Cremin (1978), the major contribution of the strategies and modes of ecology is that it identifies the complexity of educational situations and scales. In addition, it is a good way of evaluating issues in education with the theories of association, balance, and dynamics of ecology. In 1980s, Goodlad (1987) put forward his theory that a school or college is a cultural ecological system while Browers (1990) studied a series of issues related to ecology of education, such as the micro ecology (namely, the classroom teaching practice), cultural and ecological crisis, etc. (cited in Fan, 2005). In recent years, works on the ecology of education in ELT (English Language Teaching) have been published, including Tudor's *The Dynamics of the Language Classroom* (2001), Leather's *Ecology of Language Acquisition* (2003) (cited in Liu, 2008), and Garner and Borg's "An Ecological Perspective on Content-based Instruction" (2005) etc., symbolizing the gradual formation of the ecological classroom teaching of foreign languages, especially English.

The introduction of the concept of ecology of education into China started in 1980s and developed with a rapid pace. Li (1980) reflects on the issues and problems in the education of Taiwan with the application of ecology. Wu (1990) touches upon the concept and discusses the basic principles, the ecology of culture, education, educational resources, the ecological environment of schools and classrooms, as well as sustainable development. Ren (1992) tries to analyze the phenomena in education with the employment of the ideas and methods of ecology (cited in He, 2005). Fan (2000) develops a comprehensive discussion of the ecology of education from the perspectives of culture, population, resources, and environment. With the revolution in college English teaching in China spreading in 2002, teachers, educators and experts attach increasing importance to this concept to promote the revolution in college English teaching and the advancement of teaching level. Chen (2008), along with other educators, holds that the teaching environment in ELT should be "ecologized" and that the integration of computers and internet with teaching is the key to a new mode in ELT, which becomes a major part in college English teaching revolution. At the same time, Liu (2008) and Cao (2011) summarize the development of the ecology of education in ELT in China and propose the content, strategies, and design of ecological classroom in ELT.

6.2 Essential Content of Ecology of Education in ELT

According to Liu (2008), the core concern of the ecology of education is the growing of individuals and groups. As the organisms or individuals involved in education are teachers and students, the goal of the ecology of education is to build a benign relationship between the ecological subjects of students and teachers and to create an ecological environment that is beneficial to the healthy and positive development of students as individuals and groups in this environment. From an ecological perspective, and under the circumstances of the study on the integration of internet and information technology and English language teaching in the Bologna process in European countries and the rest of the world, in order to achieve such a goal, the essential content of the ecology of education in ELT could be understood in the following three ways: the ecological approach to studying language, the classroom ecology, namely, the ecological relationship between individual behaviors and the environment in the context of schools or classrooms, and the integration of computer and internet technologies and English language teaching.

6.2.1 Ecological Approach to the Study of Language

Interpreted in a narrow sense, the basic focus of ecology is on the relationship between biological organisms and the environment they are living and developing in. When applied to other disciplines, in a broader sense, ecology is about the individuals and their context as well as the relationship and interactions between the individuals and their context. Therefore, ecology provides new points of view in various disciplines, language included, and the application of the theories and notions of ecology transforms people's interpretation and study of the nature of language. According to Garner and Borg (2005), an ecological study of language endows it with three features: holistic, dynamic and interactive, and situated.

(1) Holistic Language

Language is more than a system of rules that learners need to follow; it is also a whole organism with its own systems of components, process, diversity, and interaction. Through an ecological lens, the language rules and its complex systems constitute the language itself; moreover, the different and interactive characteristics of those rules and systems continuously define the language system, with the latter regarded as the context of this organic whole. In addition, as a toolof communication, the use of a language involves diverse skills at the same time, and the communication cannot happen unless the user of language is immersed in the context of language by using his or her language skills simultaneously. Therefore, the notion of an ecological study of language contents that any aspect of language—for example, the correct grammar used in a passage or the coherence of any essay—is inseparable from other aspects or their language context, and the user of language cannot understand or produce this aspect of language without referring to or interacting with the whole language context.

(2) Dynamic and Interactive Language

It is self-evident that the development of the science of ecology is dynamic; in other words, each individual involved in an ecological system is continuously interacting with other individuals as well as the environment within which they exist and develop, and their interactions constantly create or transform the environment, or the context. Likewise, from an ecological perspective on language, its purpose of communication is more than the mere transferring of messages among people. It involves the participation of people who are using language to communicate. For example, the successful communication between people should be based on an agreement of their understanding and interpretation of the same information, and there should be exchanges of ideas and negotiations and compromises between people in order to fulfil the communication. Therefore, the use of language is a dynamic process involving the interactions between people who use the language and the interactions between people and the language context.

(3) Situated language

Employed by people to convey ideas, the usage of language can be subjective, and it is grounded in diverse situations. The way how a message is delivered or an idea is uttered depends on a wide range of factors. For instance, language is an outcome of human activities, and it is incessantly molded and changed by its social and cultural environment. The application of language by people varies because people, as the participants of communication with language as the tool, have different perceptions, perspectives, standpoints, and intentions. The process of communication with language is also determined and changed by the relationship between the participants of the conversation. The diverse media of communication, in the modern society, also alter the usage of language. Thereby, from an ecological point of view, the study of language can never be isolated from its physical settings and the social and cultural background.

6.2.2 Classroom Ecology in ELT

The concepts of ecology are the tool to guide the scientific development of the teaching activities in college English classrooms. On the one hand, the theories of ecology of education can be employed to generate a better understanding of the relationship between the ecological language environment and the factors involved in college English classes, and thus an effective approach to studying the teaching activities of ELT. On the other hand, the theories can be meaningfully put into practice and converted to strategies to improve college English teaching.

Since the ecological system refers to the relationship between the organisms and between the organisms and their living environment, the key concepts involved are systems, balance, and association. Thereby, the classroom ecology refers to the re-definition of the class activities from a perspective of ecology, and the ecology of education is mainly about the relationship between students and teachers as two major subjects of this ecological system. Their relationship should be based on a mutual respect and collaboration. Meanwhile, the teaching process should be diversified and flexible, creating an open, integrated, and sustainable learning environment for students. In other words, the classroom ecology means, under the guidance of the dynamic and sustainable development of the ecological educational concepts, to adjust the roles of teachers and students to make them both the subjects of teaching practice, to innovate teachers' teaching concepts and methods, and to promote the cultivation and development of students' independence, autonomy, and initiative in their learning process in an ecological, friendly environment.

Liu (2008) classifies the content of the classroom ecology into several major categories: (1) The ecological environment in college ELT classrooms. It refers to all the environmental elements influencing the students' and teachers' activities involved in the teaching process, namely, the ecological system including the material environment of the classroom, the systematic environment, and the cultural environment, which affects directly or indirectly the living and developing of the individuals and groups (namely, students and teachers) in the classroom. It also refers to the factors influencing students and teachers in the classroom. (2) The ecological features of the college ELT ecological classroom. To be more specific, it means the adjustment of individuals and groups to the classroom ecological environment as well as their growth and development, and the balance and imbalance of the factors constituting the classroom ecological environment due to the incessant interactions between classroom individuals or groups, thus achieving a harmonious situation. (3) In the classroom ecological environment, there are constant collaborative and competitive interactions between the individuals or groups, namely, the students, which in turn contributes to the balance and imbalance among them. (4) The positive ecological learning and teaching environment with computer and internet integrated. (5) The evaluation and supervision system in the ecological college English teaching classroom, which attaches importance to the classroom activities, teachers' teaching behaviors, students' development, and the ecological environment in which they are interacting. In the Bologna Process, many a university in European countries adopts the concept so that students are immersed in their interactions with other students and with teachers either in or outside classroom, creating a harmonious learning environment.

6 - 1 **Cardiff University of the UK**

6 - 2 **University of Minnesota Rochester**

In a word, through the lens of ecology, the college English education is an organic integration of the ecological subjects—both teachers and students—and the teaching ecological environment, namely, the material environment and the spiritual environment. The spiritual environment includes elements such as the teaching concepts, content, systems, classroom culture, emotional bond between teachers and students, etc. while the material environment refers to teaching time, location, and the relevant teaching facilities used in English teaching, which, to a large extent, means multimedia and internet information technology.

6.2.3 Organic Integration of Information Technology and College English Teaching in Bologna Process

With the advancement of science and technology, the science of ecology is gradually being assimilated into other disciplines, promoting the integration of theoretical researches on ecology and the applied study. In the new era of information technology, the introduction of computers and internet into education has shown its advantage in teaching innovation. The year of 2001 witnessed the national revolution in college English teaching in China. Later on in 2004, the department of education promulgated a document as the guidance for this revolution, which stated that the essential part of the innovation is the multimedia teaching mode of foreign languages based on computers and classroom teaching, which is also known as CAI (Computer-assisted Instruction) and CAL (Computer-assisted Learning) (Chen, 2006). Along the Bologna Process, the universities in many European counties, especially in Switzerland, have attached great importance to the information technology and bring it into teaching and learning process. The integration of modern technology into teaching practice gives scope to its advantage: the interactions and collaboration with elements of ELT promote their mutual development and create a natural and harmonious ecological environment for language teaching and learning in colleges. According to Chen, however, ELT with the assistance of computers and internet is not the ultimate goal; the key to achieve a real innovated teaching mode is to switch the role of computers and internet applied to college English classroom teaching from the assistance to an indispensable component. That is, computer and internet technology should be integrated into English teaching to achieve an ecological teaching environment.

6 - 3 **Franklin University, Switzerland**

6 - 4 **University of Rennes, France**

In recent years, computer technology has entered college English teaching classroom and played a significant role in English teachers' teaching practice. However, traditional teaching mode is called "computer-assisted teaching", which means teachers resort to computer and internet technology in their teaching practice and ameliorate their teaching methods and improve the teaching effects with the assistance of some functions or software of the computer. For example, teachers use computers to display PowerPoints in class as a way to assist in communicating teaching content or play videos or audios to diversify the methods of teaching language. With the assistance of some teaching platforms and software, students can review the class content after the learning activities in class are over, which contributes to the cultivation of students' self-learning ability and initiative.

The assisting function of computers, however, is mainly about some manipulation and exercise software, and the objects that the computers assist are teachers and their functions can only get displayed through the operation of teachers (Chen, 2006). Nevertheless, these functions of computers are only working for consolidating the knowledge students have already learnt, but not for helping students acquire new knowledge, and encourage the old way of learning English by memorizing (Morrison & Lowther, 2005). Therefore, computers as a technology can only assist teachers to improve the teaching effect, to some degree, but cannot be a tool for teachers to solve the practical problems in their teaching activities (Morrison & Lowther, 2005).

Therefore, in order to create an ecological learning environment for English language students, it is not enough to resort to computers and internet as assistance. The role ofthe computer as assistance actually undermines the function and power of its own, and contributes little for an ideal ecological learning environment for students. On the contrary, if teachers could create a simulated virtual language environment with modern information technology, students may learn and practice the target language in that simulated virtual environment, which makes the integration of language teaching and the information technology with the computer and internet as its core.

6.3 Impediments on the Way to Ecology of Education in ELT

During any teaching or learning process in any country, teachers, students, content, and classroom are the basic elements. With the accumulation of teaching experiences of a long history, traditional modes of English teaching as second or foreign language have enjoyed popularity over the years under the guidance of mature theories and principles. However, from an ecological perspective, as is discussed above, language is not static, but dynamic and situated, which requires the teaching and learning of a language to adapt to the ever changing social and cultural environment. Especially in the era of information, modern technology or internet has been assimilated in people's work, study, and life. The changing life style demands the modification of teaching and learning style to achieve the optimum effects. An ecological way of ELT is thus in need to ensure that the development of ELT in college fits the dynamic factors of the organic individuals and groups as well as their environment, namely, teachers, students, classroom, community, society, etc. However, on the way to striving for ecology of education in ELT in many countries, there are quite a few obstacles or problems to be solved, among which the following three are worth more attention.

6.3.1 The Isolation of Language from Its Environment

From an ecological perspective, not only should language be examined by referring to its social and cultural context, but the learning of language cannot be separated from the environment in which this language is employed, and the different language skills of reading, writing, speaking, listening, argument, etc. should be inseparable components in the process of language learning. In a word, the environment within which the language is used plays a significant role in one's learning of the language.

However, take the English learners in China for example, in the past several decades, there was a common phenomenon called "deaf English" or "dumb English". Most English learners did not have a good command of listening and speaking skills, the reason of which was, confined by the language environment, they did not have many opportunities to practice or use their listening and speaking skills. Compared with China, English learners from European countries and some other Asian countries, such as India, Singapore, Philippine, etc., have stronger communicative ability. One of the causes, according to Chen (2006), is that English is second language for them while it is a foreign language for Chinese learners, and there is a huge distinction between learning and using English as second language and as a foreign language in the aspects of language functions, the way and purpose of learning the language as well as the language environment. In the countries where English is second language, it is used in a wide range of contexts of the society, including education, culture, politics, business, entertainment, etc., in which the learners are fully immersed in the language environment and can thus quickly improve their language proficiency in all of the four aspects. In countries where English is a foreign language, however, English is only learnt and used in classroom rather than in everyday life. With teachers and textbooks as the major resources of the language, the chance that English learners are exposed in an English language environment is limited. In addition, different learning environments result in varied learning motives and methods. For those learning English as second language, they need to have a high proficiency of the language in order to meet the challenges and competitions from work and life and to survive in the society. Learning English is not an advantage but a necessity. Nevertheless, in China, although English learning has been attached increasing importance to, the motive of most learners is still to pass exams or to obtain a certificate or a diploma, which makes the acquisition of language knowledge all the more important in order to pass exams. Consequently, the communicative skills of listening and speaking are neglected. What is worse, the ELT in schools is accordingly steered from the cultivation of language skills in practical application to the command of theoretical knowledge. The isolation of the learning and use of language from its environment thus goes against the ecological notion of language and language learning and poses as an obstacle to the achievement of ecological ELT.

6.3.2 Imbalance of Classroom Ecology in ELT

In the natural ecological environment, the ecological balance refers to the state of consistency and mutual adaptation between biological individuals, groups and between the organisms and their environment through the flow of energy, circulation of substances, and communication of information in an ecological system (Fan, 1999). Keeping balance within an ecological system is crucial to a healthy and positive ecological environment which is suitable for the organisms to live within. From an ecological point of view, likewise, composed of natural environment, social and cultural environment, and the values, a college English classroom is a complicated ecological environment, which is constantly created and transformed by the interactions among individuals or groups and their interactions with their environment. However, generally speaking, the imbalance of these elements may cause the imbalance within such an ecological environment, which needs the organisms—namely, teachers and students—to pay attention to.

(1) Imbalance between Ecological Subjects

The ecological subjects refer to teachers and students who are involved in teaching activities. Teachers and students are equal subjects in their teaching and learning practice, and their interactions in and outside class as well as their mutual feedback on each other's performance collaborate to work out better teaching and learning theories and strategies, thus achieving the optimum classroom effects. In traditional ELT classroom, however, teachers play the leading role and are regarded as the subjects that control the class. Students, on the contrary, passively receive the teaching content which is more about language knowledge rather than the cultivation of language skills and capabilities. Such imbalance between the subjects leads to students' incompetence in applied skills of language and impedes students' development of autonomy and initiative in learning.

Besides, the static and limited teaching approaches and methods are another element causing the imbalance between teachers and students in ELT. In countries where English is studied asa second or foreign language, classroom teaching is still the dominating form of language acquisition. However, students' language skills and capabilities differ from one another, and are in constant progress as time goes by, which thereby requires teachers to adopt diverse teaching strategies and approaches, constantly reflect on and evaluate their teaching behaviors and effects, and revise their teaching concepts and methods. Otherwise, teachers' teaching ideas and methods will fail to be suitable for students and result in the imbalance between them.

A case study of in Denmark (Rubdy, 2000), though about an in-service program for teachers of English as foreign language in Denmark offered by British trainers, also reflects the subjects' dilemma in the ecological environment of teaching-learning process. In this case, the British trainers are teachers while the Danish teachers of English are learners. In the first and second phases of the training program, the trainers played the role of "experts" and the main source of knowledge and theory on communicative English language teaching, and the program turned out to be of limited value, exerting little impact on the classroom. Later on, as the trainers reflected on their approaches and incorporated major changes in training which encouraged the learners to display their autonomy, initiative, and innovation in their classrooms as teachers, more fruitful effects were achieved. Instead of being the objects of the transmission of the trainers' knowledge and skills, the learners become independent agents actively receiving, internalizing, and utilizing the knowledge and skills. Therefore, a balance between the teaching subjects and learning subjects is crucial in the learning process. Positioning the learners as the focal point of the classroom activity adjusts the relationship between teachers and learners to be interdependent and reciprocal.

(2) Imbalance between Ecological Subjects and Their Environment

The environment within which the ecological subjects live and develop, when applied to ELT, refers to the classroom ecology where the teaching and learning activities take place. One reason for the imbalance between the ecological subjects (teachers and students) and their environment (the classroom, community, or even the society) is the large scale of classes when English is being taught. Language, as a tool, needs to be applied and practiced through communication between participants, or language learners; however, in some public universities in the United States as well as in China, for example, the number of students in ELT class can be as big as 45 to 90 (Liu, 2008), which exceeds the tolerance of the resources in this ecological system and goes against the optimum standard in the ecology of education. Such imbalance between subjects and environment will also lead to the scarcity of teaching resources allocated to each student and the increase of biological and mental pressure students may feel.

Another factor leading to the imbalance between the learning subjects and the environment is the exam-oriented education system. Standardized tests require students' output of language knowledge mainly through reading and writing and neglected the cultivation of students' practical language skills and listening and speaking, which goes against the value of education and holds back the comprehensive development of students' language skills and capability.

An insufficient language environment is also one cause of the imbalance. A learning environment should be suitable for students and meet their need of practicing the language and strengthening their ability to use the language through communication. However, in many ELT teaching practice, a lack of extracurricular language environment outside the classroom will eventually result in the imbalance between in-class learning and after-class practicing, and subsequently lead to the imbalance between the learning subjects and their ecological environment within which they could achieve better learning effects.

6.3.3 "Computer-assisted" ELT

In the new era of increasingly advanced information technology, ELT calls for the new teaching mode based on the integration of computers and college English teaching. Under the circumstances of the Bologna process, internet education prevails in most countries, and teaching and learning practice starts to be integrated with computers and internet to achieve better teaching and learning effects, which is the reflection of the concepts and principles of creating an ecological learning environment.

According to Chen (2006), with the development of computer and internet technology, CAI (Computer-assisted Instruction) was firstly applied to foreign language teaching during 1950s to 1980s, with its major function of demonstrating teaching content in the forms of pictures, animations, and simulation. During 1980s to 1990s, with the revolution in foreign language teaching from the teacher-centered trend to the students-centered, CAL (Computer-assisted Learning) came into being as a tool to assist students to review teachers' teaching content or make learning plans, thus promoting students' development of self-learning ability and initiative in study. The key word of both terms, however, is "assist", which means it helps teachers and students in their teaching or learning, and their functions is only displayed by the operation of the teaching or learning subjects. For example, the function of CAI is to refine teachers' teaching effects in class, which is characterized with the facts that (1) teachers are the leading subjects in teaching-learning activities; (2) it is no more than a demonstrative tool to help teachers diverse their teaching methods; and (3) the teaching content and structure remain the same. Therefore, the assistance of computers is only to reinforce the teaching effects, but cannot solve the practical problems in teaching practice (Morrison & Lowther, 2005).

Therefore, there are limitations of using computers in ELT as assistance. For instance, the mode of CAI considers computers as a tool instead of an organic component of the teaching process of college English, and thus the computers lose the advantage of combining with internet or other information technologies to achieve the optimum effects by making the most of various teaching resources. Therefore, using the computer as an assisting tool to strengthen the classroom teaching effects undermines the display of its huge potential, which contributes little to creating an ideal, ecological environment for teachers and students.

In a nutshell, in college English teaching-learning practice, with joint efforts of teachers and students, a contextual environment that is appropriate to teachers' teaching practice and students' learning activities should be created. Educators and teachers should take into consideration diverse elements that may influence the relationships between them and students and the interactions between both subjects and their environment to achieve the optimum teaching and learning effects.

6.4 Applying Ecology of Education to ELT

The essential content of ecology is the system, balance, and interaction. In other words, an ecological system should be composed of organisms which interact with each other and interact with the environment in order to achieve the mutual development in the endless process of balance and imbalance. The birth and development of language is based on the communicative and cultural environment in which language is used. The environment of language may include several different aspects: the ecological subjects (namely, teachers and students), the institution in which the language is taught, the principles and standard on which language is used, and the interactions between ecological subjects and between subjects and the discourse community, such as the school and the classroom. Therefore, in order to create a balanced and harmonious ecological environment for college English language teaching, educators, teachers, and institutions of education should adopt strategies to keep the balance in the ecological teaching system in college English classes, achieve the effective association and interaction within the classroom, and promote teachers' teaching effects and students' progressive development of English proficiency. Creating a healthy ecological teaching system should be based on the three basic elements involved in the ecological system of college English teaching: teachers, students, and the classroom and community environment.

6.4.1 Teachers as Ecological Subjects

In face-to-face classroom teaching-learning process, teachers play a significant role in carrying out teaching activities. Thereby, in the ecological system of college English teaching, teachers, as one of the major ecological subjects, determine, to some extent, whether the language environment is healthy and ecological enough for students' language acquisition. In order to achieve this goal, teachers should plan for classes reasonably, adopt the teaching strategies and approaches that fit the particular teaching content and objects, evaluate their teaching performance by assessing students' performance in and outside class as well as paying attention to students' doubts and constructive feedback on class activities, adjust and even change the traditional teaching plan and practice in order to receive better teaching effects in the future teaching activities. Based on this principle, teachers should attach great importance to the following four aspects in order to fulfil their task of being ecological subjects to guarantee an ecological system of a benign circulation.

(1) Systematic and Scientific Teaching Ideas

A healthy ecological language teaching-learning system requires subjects of equal relationships interacting incessantly to achieve a reciprocal, co-existing situation. Therefore, it is especially profound for teachers to possess more scientific teaching ideas which stress students' position as subjects rather than objects, and guide them to give full play of their autonomy and initiative. In the teaching process, besides imparting language skills and knowledge directly, teachers also need to offer guidance to students to discover their own problems in the language learning process and encourage students to figure out solutions which are the most effective and suitable. Consequently, students can gain a better understanding of the language knowledge as well as the strategies for independent study, which lays a solid foundation for their future study and the establishment of their own knowledge system.

(2) Reasonable Teaching Objective

Under the guidance of a set of scientific and reasonable teaching ideas and concepts, the setting up of reasonable teaching objective before class is equally essential for teachers to display their active role as ecological subjects in the ecological system of ELT. In recent years, with the innovation in language teaching, the traditional teaching mode has been switched from teacher-centered to student-centered, and the teaching objective is also shifted from the passing on of language knowledge to the cultivation of students' self-learning ability with strong autonomy and initiative. Consequently, the range of teachers' roles has been greatly expanded, covering instructor, advisor, guide, evaluator, supervisor, etc. and the teaching objective, in a narrower sense, should be steered to creating the environment for students to actively find problems and solve the problems on their own, as well as develop the habit of learning independently and creatively, so that students will be better immersed in the language learning culture and their interests in learning English will be greatly stimulated.

(3) Appropriate Teaching Content

With the innovation in teaching ideas and objective, the teaching content should be adjusted accordingly to meet the requirements of new objectives. The teaching plan should be adapted to be more suitable for cultivating students' language skills and capabilities of learning English by themselves under the guidance of teachers. In addition, more original and authentic English language materials of various styles should be introduced as supplementary teaching resources in English classes, such as magazines, newspapers, literary works, video and audio materials, etc. This broadens students' horizon in reading and listening materials, exposes students to more diverse yet authentic language resources, and encourages students to learn and practice the language initiatively.

Another important issue about teaching content is the impromptu display of teachers' language proficiency in knowledge and skills. Teaching is like improvising a performance filled with unexpected incidents, and teachers constantly get inspired by the results of class discussion, students' questions, and interactions between students and between students and teachers, and may initiate further discussion in the related topics which will greatly benefit students. Such teaching content is not prepared by teachers in advance but is closely related to the subject of a text, more usages of a vocabulary words, or students' problems, needs, and interests in English learning, and the discussion of this aspect of teaching content will be undoubtedly beneficial to students' broadened horizon, capability of thinking more in-depth, and aspiration for a better command of English. Therefore, teachers should never stop enriching their own knowledge bank and teaching methods and be prepared for the unexpected teaching content and questions arising in ELT classrooms.

(4) Reflective Teaching Attitude

Reflective teaching has been a well-accepted teaching concept and mode around the world in ELT. It is a crucial stepin teaching process that teachers reflect constantly on their teaching ideas, plans, contents, methods, and teaching performances before, during, or after the teaching practice, evaluate the teaching effects, and adjust each link of the whole process. An actively and constantly reflective teacher is most likely to display his or her potentials for becoming a positive ecological subject that is beneficial to every component of the ecological system of ELT for mainly two reasons. One reason is that reflection is an extension of teaching activities, which is of great prominence to teachers' summary of their teaching experiences, feedback on teaching activities, and the evaluation of teaching behaviors and effects. The other contributing factor is that the results of reflection can be transformed into teaching experience and theory, which will function as guidance for the future teaching plan and practice and be valuable for teachers' advanced teaching capacity and professional development.

6.4.2 Students as Ecological Subjects

In order to promote students' role as subjects, instead of objects in traditional English teaching concepts, in the ecological system of ELT, teachers should abandon the old teaching mode of imparting language knowledge only with students passively receiving knowledge and should adopt innovative teaching approaches in order to cultivate students' ability to learn independently and collaborate in study and to gradually foster the academic spirits of researching, sharing, and exchanging among students. Generally, three most effective ways can be adopted to achieve this goal.

(1) Fostering Students' Initiative and Creativity in English Learning

In an ecological system, the subjects are incessantly interacting with one another and with their environment. Such symbiotic and competitive interactions advance the evolution of the ecological subjects in the process of alternate balance and imbalance. English teaching, therefore, should also be based on the collaborative and competitive interactions between students in order to achieve better learning effects and the mutual improvement of the interacting students. There are three types of goals that can motivate students' study (cited in Liu, 2008). One is the individual goal, that is, the learners believe that they should be independent in study in order to achieve their goals. Another type is competitive goal, which means the learners hold that they are able to beat other learners to achieve their own study goals. The third one is called collaborative goal that the learners believe they and other learners can both achieve with cooperation. These three types of goals reflect the optimum relationship between the learning subjects, namely, the students, in the ecological system of English learning.

Creativity and productivity are achieved through cooperation and competition; likewise, students can develop their creativity, autonomy, and initiative in English study through the symbiotic and competitive interactions with one another. For example, when assigned a project, students can work in groups to collaborate in conducting researches, having discussions, preparing for presentations and stage plays, etc. and each group can compete with one another in various forms, like speech contests or debates. Such kinds of class activities can motivate students' aspiration for independent research and study and help them cultivate the awareness of competition and teamwork spirits.

(2) Enriching Students' Resources in English Learning through Diverse Media

With the ceaseless advancement of computer and internet technology, various free web resources for learning English become available, which not only greatly enrich the teaching materials for English teachers but also provide students with better platforms to conduct independent study. For example, some online writing websites possess the function of grading essays automatically. Therefore, students may submit their essays to be graded by the system and get suggestions for revision. Besides, such online systems also provide English dictionary and language corpus so that students can enlarge their vocabulary bank and learn common collocations to write more authentic English expressions. Some applications that can be downloaded and installed in students' computers or smart phones can also help students learn more information about English language usages and exchange ideas with others online about study approaches or experience, etc., which improves students' language skills in various ways. Such internet sources facilitate students' development of the ability of self-learning and self-evaluation. In addition, students should expose themselves in the language learning environment with the assistance of other media. For instance, students can develop the habit of listening to English news broadcast or watch English TV programs and reading authentic English newspapers, magazines, novels to improve their listening and reading ability. Besides, teachers should also encourage students to organize and participate in English speech contests, debates, or plays on the campus so as to practice public speaking skills in English. Thus, under the guidance of teachers, abundant internet resources contribute to cultivating students' ability to study independently with initiative as active subjects in the ecological system of ELT.

(3) Evaluating and Encouraging Students' Performance in Learning Process

Students' grades in quizzes and tests should not be the only criterion for assessing their ability or performance in a learning process. Other elements need to be taken into consideration when regarding the whole learning process as an ecological system constituted by the interactions between the subjects and between subjects and their environment and other elements including students' motive and interest in study, feedback and reflection on their own and teachers' performance, the remaining questions after teachers' teaching process, and the improvements they have made compared with their performances prior to the present one.

Another issue that needs attention is that the evaluation and encouragement should be positive and vary from student to student. Students' language proficiency varies, and thus the criteria for evaluating each student should be distinct. With the evaluation and feedback given by teachers, students will have a better understanding of their own language proficiency and problems and gain more confidence through tackling the problems and improving their language skills. Therefore, teachers should conduct positive, encouraging evaluations based on the particular situation and language proficiency of each student.

6.4.3 Classroom and Community Ecological Environment

There is no evolution or development of an organism without its constant interactions with other species and the environment within which it exists. In the ecological system of college ELT, likewise, an appropriate and reasonable language environment is an essential element in students' development of language skills. Based on ecology of education, three approaches can be adopted to create an ecological language environment that is suitable for college English learners.

(1) Small-scale Classes and Study Groups

According to the principles of ecology, like any other ecological system, there is a limit on the tolerance of resources and capacity of the environment within college English classroom system. Therefore, a limit on the population of students in an English class is of great significance for the achievement of better teaching and learning effects. The way to study English, a language, is through constant accumulation and practice; the improvement of communicative skills, namely, listening and speaking skills, is accomplished mainly through one-to-one communication, thus requiring a smaller class and less dense population. In addition, according to ecology, when a class is divided into several study groups, they will display differences; the differences lead to competition, and competition promotes common advancement of the groups. Such symbiotic and competitive relationship between ecological subjects is the essential condition for more efficient allocation of resources, stronger vitality of the ecological system, and the achievement of sustainable development of ecological subjects (Fan, 1999).

(2) Balance of Knowledge Acquirement and Skill Development

A student-friendly ecological learning environment is not merely for students to passively receive language knowledge from teachers. Instead, the major target of college ELT classes is to cultivate and develop students' language capability either individually or in a group, and thereby teachers should work together with students to create a language environment which is of great help for students to put language knowledge into practice and gradually ameliorate their language proficiency in formal and informal communications. Therefore, keeping the balance between the acquirement of language knowledge and the cultivation of practice language skills is crucial for the establishment and maintenance of an ecological environment for ELT.

(3) EcologicalEnvironment of ELT

According to the ideas of ecology, any ecological system must be open to the exchange of energy and information with the outside world in order to survive and grow. The language teaching system is of no exception as an ecological system as well. Therefore, the small ecological environment of college English classroom is no longer sufficient to provide the authentic language environment and situations for students to practice their language skills. As Shan (2007) indicates, college English teachers should break the traditional classroom limitations of time and space, extend the classroom to the community and even the society, guide students to be exposed to the more open ecological system, reinforce the association between the in-class study and outside-class practice, and stress the interactions between the classroom teaching and the outside society in order to ensure students to achieve better learning effects.

An EAP (English for Academic Purposes) program set up in Northumbria University in the UK embodies the concept of building an appropriate English language learning environment (Garner & Borg, 2005). Teachers from English Language Center of Northumbria University are dedicated to providing a language environment in which contextual conditions are created based on the situation of the learners and are proper for the learners to embrace the language as a common discourse that they can understand and use. Therefore, they develop an academic communicative link which teachers and students are actively involved in during their own academic processes within the discourse community and is thus like the environment in which they learn and practice English language. For example, the teachers choose global issues as the context for international students learning English as second or foreign language. With a wide coverage of world issues such as technological innovation, economic changes, and the influence of globalization on local culture, global issues become a topic that most students can discuss and receive relevant content. The teachers are carefully selected, who have rich experiences of learning and teaching this topic and are able to connect one topic to another in order to create an intellectual environment to discuss the issues critically as well as linguistically. In fact, this environmental framework helps build the communicative links in the language classroom, and English language learners become more easily adapted to new contexts, such as listening to lectures in their subject areas or finishing writing tasks in a certain discipline, than those who are only engaged with the basic grammar rules and contexts of traditional language learning, thus achieving the effect of learning and using the language in a broader ecological environment.

6 – 5 **Northumbria University, UK**

6 – 6 **Library of Northumbria University**

6.4.4 Integration of Computer and Internet Technologies and ELT

Today, the computer and internet technologies are widely used in almost every aspect of human life, such as education, business, politics, health, etc. In education, for example, multimedia and internet technologies have facilitate teachers and educators of all disciplines to improve the quality of their teaching practice and increase the achievements in their professional development. In the teaching and learning of English language, in particular, the computer and internet technologies have brought about great revolution; computer software, websites, projectors, radio, recorders, etc. have been at the disposal of English language teachers in many colleges and become indispensable tools for teachers to deliver language knowledge, train students' language skills, and cultivate their ability to learn independently.

However, as Sharndama (2013) argues, the information and communication technologies do not themselves transform the ideas or approaches to the teaching and learning of English language. It is the appropriate application of these technologies by teachers that does the job. In addition, Chen (2006) points out that there is an essential distinction between computer-assisted teaching and the integration of computer and internet technologies and English teaching. In other words, computer-assisted teaching stresses the function of assistance, which means the technologies help teachers in their teaching methods and strategies in order to reinforce the teaching effects. However, the integration emphasizes that the computer and internet technologies have become an indispensable ecological component of teaching practice. Higgins (1995) indicates that the main value of computer and internet technologies is to function as an environment in which the ecological subjects of language learners and teachers interact to carry out language activities and experiments (cited in Barani, 2014). Therefore, with the training of language skills and self-learning ability and the passing on of language knowledge remaining equally important, the integration of computer and internet technologies and English language teaching makes it possible for teachers to transform their teaching strategies and methods in order to create a student-centered learning environment instead of the traditional teacher-centered one which has been prevailing for long. According to Chen (2006), this integration will transform the nature of English teaching mainly in two aspects.

(1) Abandoning the Traditional Classroom-textbook Teaching Mode

In traditional English language teaching classroom, the communication between teachers and students is mostly one-way: teachers function as the dominating subjects, conveying language knowledge to students with textbooks as the media while students, as the objects of teaching, passively receive the knowledge through reading textbooks and teachers' analysis and explanation. Even with the assistance of computer software and internet, for example, teachers use PowerPoints to communicate the language knowledge from the textbooks or play video and audio clips related to the topic of that particular lesson. Still, such assistance merely varies the forms of delivering language knowledge and reinforces, to some extent, the teaching effects, but cannot change or abandon the limitation of the teacher-centered teaching mode and the one-way communication between teachers and students.

With the integration of computer and internet technologies and English teaching, however, more elements related to teaching practice are involved and interact with each other, including the teacher, students, classroom, computer, and textbook. The relationship among these elements is no longer teacher-centered; instead, each of them is interactive with, interdependent on, and inter-transformative to one another. Students, no long the teaching objects, become the active constructors of their language knowledge. Furthermore, the utilization of computer and internet technologies also brings abundant English learning resources and thus broadens students' scope of knowledge, and students can give full play of their learning autonomy in choosing to internalize and employ this knowledge.

(2) Creating an Ecological English Teaching and Learning Environment

According to Kenning and Kenning (1883), the essential advantage of the computer as a medium for education over other modern technological equipment, such as film projectors and tape recorders, lies in its capability of interacting with the teaching and learning subjects. The communication of textbooks and tape recording with students is one-way, telling students what the rules are, what language points they need to remember, and what the solutions to problems are, but cannot evaluate students' learning behaviors and performance, analyze the specific mistake that a student has made, and guide the student to find out not only how to correct his or her mistake but also why it is a mistake and what he or she should do in order to find a solution and prevent similar mistakes in future study. With the dramatic advancement of computer and internet technologies, the integration of these technologies and English language teaching has become possible and accelerated the creation of an ecological teaching and learning environment which guarantees the student-centered English teaching and learning mode.

For instance, combining sounds, images, and texts which draw students' attention and interest, some multimedia computer software provides real life situations for learners to be engaged in the English learning process and interact with various learning texts to improve their English language proficiency (Sharndama, 2013). Some vocabulary software incorporates video, audio recording, and graphics to diversify the learning content. Some more sophisticated error-checking software gives feedback to learners and helps them analyze the feedback to direct them to further and more complicated practice. In writing, as well, some online programs provide students with guidelines on the generation of the outline and main ideas in the pre-writing period, evaluate students' writing in every aspect, and give feedback and revising suggestions. In addition, some pronunciation programs also have the function of comparing the recording of students' oral practice and the model voice for students to find out and work on their problems in further study. Most computer programs are designed to stimulate students to discuss after either their learning practice or evaluation to facilitate students' development of critical thinking, and many practice questions also incorporate games and competitions to add more fun and excitement to students' practice and to get them more actively involved. These computer software or programs focus on the interactions among students, computer and internet, and language knowledge and skills, thereby creating an appropriate, positive, and pleasant learning environment to maximize students' learning enthusiasm and effects (Barani, 2014).

In other words, therefore, an ideal, ecological language teaching environment should be one of student-centered, which means, students acquire knowledge and skills not by mechanical imitation or memorization, but by comprehending and internalizing; students should be equipped with the ability to connect what they have learnt with what they need to learn; students should attach importance to constant assessment on their own performance in order to achieve more personal improvements. With the integration of computer and internet technologies and English learning, the ideal, ecological language teaching and learning environment should contain three types of teaching and learning modes (Chen, 2006):

—Situational study. English, as a language, is employed to communicate in everyday, real situations; however, in traditional English teaching mode, language study is based on textbooks and in the classroom and is thus isolated from situations. With the integration of computer technologies and English study, a virtual, emulated situation can be easily created online, such as a restaurant, a fitness center, or a bank where students can experience these situations and practice relevant language expressions flexibly. Such a situation created by computer technologies generates a reality-like language learning environment where the learning subjects, namely, the students, interact with each other and with the environment.

—Collaborative study. The collaboration in an ecological English learning environment refers to the cooperation between students and between students and teachers. A teacher transforms his or her role from the leading subject to a member of the students' study group, which helps promote the interactions, cooperation, and competition among students. The integration makes it possible to reinforce such collaboration. For instance, new and advanced online teaching systems provide opportunities for teachers and students to interact by sending e-mails and messages online and discussing in blogs, online forums, and discussion groups. Students can also collaborate to work on projects with the utilization of computer software and programs.

—Open study. Distinguished from traditional teaching mode which chooses and communicates the teaching content mainly by teachers' imparting, a student-centered, open learning environment requires students to choose the learning content according to their own condition and language proficiency. With rich internet resources and learning software available, students utilize the computer and internet to acquire, analyze, process, internalize, utilize, and assess the resources with the help and guidance of teachers, and proceed to use them to collaborate and communicate with teachers and other students to achieve the optimum learning effects.

As a positive example of integrating computer and internet technologies with English teaching, the Hong Kong curriculum encourages English teachers to use new media and popular culture to invigorate classes and motivate students, and 2L (Second Language) teachers have been trained to learn and use animation software, especially in Hong Kong Polytechnic University (DeCoursey, 2011). The learning process of animation is sufficiently communicative, offering opportunities to 2L teachers to frame class activities, learning tasks, and evaluation in all skills areas and creating an ecological language learning environment in which students are endowed with more resources and options in their English learning process.

6 – 7 **Hong Kong Polytechnic University**

6 – 8 **Library of Hong Kong Polytechnic University**

6.4.4 Conclusion of Ecology of ELT Education in Bologna Process

All the elements constituting a teaching system are interrelated and interactive. The ecology of education emphasizes the idea of harmony, association, and development in the process of education with the goal of the symbiosis of all ecological subjects and the environment which the subjects exist in and interact with. In the ecological teaching and learning system, the organisms co-exist and compete with each other and benefit from each other, in the constantly alternate state of balance and imbalance, and eventually achieve harmony.

In an ecological language teaching and learning framework, language is holistic and reflects the dynamic nature of being utilized in the real world. It is, and should be situated in a communicative context to facilitate students' development of both linguistic and intellectual abilities. In the Bologna process, on their way to achieving the ecological English language environment, college teachers from European countries and all over the world abandon the traditional ideas of teacher-centered mode of teaching, adapt themselves to various roles before, in, and after the teaching practice, integrate modern computer and internet technologies with teaching, etc., to guarantee students' cultivation of both language skills and self-learning ability and initiative. It further refines teachers' teaching ideas, approaches, and capabilities, thus achieving their sustainable professional development. The ecology of education in ELT around the world is an effective approach to the ceaseless progress of language education.

Bibliography

[1] Barani, G. Computer Assisted Language Learning in ELT Contexts [J]. Modern Journal of Language Teaching Methods, 2014 (4).

[2] Barrows, H. S. How to Design a Problem-based Curriculum for the Precinical Years [M]. New York: Springer, 1985.

[3] Cremin, L. A. Public Education [M]. New York: Basic Books, 1976.

[4] Tudor, I. The Dynamics of the Language Classroom [M]. Cambridge: Cambridge University Press, 2001.

[5] DeCoursey, C. A. Trialing Cartoons: Teachers' Attitudes towards Animation as an ELT Instructional Tool [J]. Computers & Education, 2012 (59).

[6] Garner, M., and Borg, E. An Ecological Perspective on Content-based Instruction [J]. Journal of English for Academic Purposes, 2005 (4).

[7] Kenning, M. M., and Kenning, M. J. Computers and Language Learning: Current Theory and Practice [M]. England: Ellis Horwood Limited, 1990.

[8] Leather, J., and Dam, J. V. Ecology of Language Acquisition [M].

Dordrench: Kluwer Academic Publishers, 2003 (10).

[9] Morrison, G. R and Lowther, D. L. Integrating Computer Technology into the Classroom [M]. Pearson Education Asia Limited, 2005.

[10] Rubdy, R. Dilemmas in ELT: Seeds of Discontent or Sources of Transformation? [J]. System, 2000 (28).

[11] Sharndama, E. C. Application of ICTs in Teaching and Learning English (ELT) in Large Classes [J]. System, 2003 (9).

[12] 曹路漫:《教育生态学视角下的大学英语教学策略研究》,《中国高等教育》2011 年第 8 期。

[13] 陈坚林:《大学英语教学新模式下计算机网络与外语课程的有机整合—对计算机“辅助”外语教学概念的生态学考察》,《外语电化教学》2006 年第 12 期。

[14] 范国睿:《英美教育生态综述》,《华东师范大学学报:教育科学版》1995 年第 2 期。

[15] 贺祖斌:《高等教育生态研究述评》,《广西师范大学学报(哲学社会科学版)》2005 年第 1 期。

[16] 李芳媛:《计算机网络环境下大学英语课程生态化探索》,《外语电化教学》2011 年第 7 期。

[17] 刘森林:《生态化大学英语课堂模式设计研究》,《外语电化教学》2008 年第 5 期。

[18] 单岩:《生态学视角下的大学英语课堂教学研究》,《中国成人教育》2007 年第 10 期。

注　解

1. 教育生态学(Ecology of Education):教育生态学是将教育及其所处的生态环境相联系,并以二者的相互关系及其机理为研究对象的一门新兴学科。该学科名称首先是由美国哥伦比亚师范学院院长 Lawrence Cremin 于 1976 年在其《公共教育》(*Public Education*)一书中提出的。教育生态规律是指以生态学观点来研究教育与其外部生态环境之间以及教育内部各环节、各层次之间本质、必然联系的基本规律。

2. 计算机辅助教学（Computer - assisted Instruction，简称 CAI）：是指教师在计算机辅助下进行各种教学活动的一种方法与技术。它既是计算机在教育中的重要应用领域，又代表一种新的教学理念和教学方式，解决了传统教学方式中单一、片面的问题。在计算机网络技术的辅助下，教师以对话方式与学生讨论教学内容、安排教学活动、评估教学效果等，为学生提供一个良好的个人化学习环境。CAI 同时综合运用多媒体、超文本、人工智能及知识库等计算机技术，能有效提高教师的教学质量和课堂效果，帮助学生缩短学习时间、提高学习效率，从而实现最优化的教学效果。

3. 计算机辅助学习（Computer - assisted Learning，简称 CAL）：与 CAI（计算机辅助教学）相比强调用计算机帮助“学”的方面甚于“教”的方面。总体而言，欧洲国家及美国东海岸地区偏向于 CAL 名称。

4. 学术用途英语（English for Academic Purposes，简称 EAP）：该课程通常是指英语语言国家的大学为已满足学术条件、但英语未达到要求的国际学生开设的英语桥梁课程。不同大学的 EAP 课程会有所差异。有些大学的课程是帮助学生提高英语水平与技能以适应英语语言的大学学术环境，而有些大学的课程则提供该学校某一具体学科的相关语言培训，如国际贸易、会计等。有些 EAP 课程是学生在开始学习专业课程之前为提高英语水平而选修的预科课程，有的课程则可随其他专业课程一同选修。大多数情况下，进入英语语言国家大学的留学生修完 EAP 课程后，英语水平得到提高，为进入专业课程的学习奠下良好的基础。

5. 第二语言（Second Language，简称 2L）：指人们在获得第一语言（即母语）后再学习并使用的第二种语言，通常会作为辅助性语言。第二语言的学习，往往可能是由于第一语言不再具有优势（社会变迁、政治目的等）。第二语言可以在不同的环境中获得，如课堂环境、自然环境、外语环境、二语环境等，取决于目的语被习得与使用的场所。

Chapter Seven Action Research and ELT Teachers' Professional Self-development

7.1 A Review of Action Research

7.1.1 Action Research

It can be seen that action research is a kind of research in which ELT teachers engage themselves in professional development in classroom based on action research. The earliest use is in the forties of the 20th century by the A-merican collier J. Collier and Lewin K. Lewin who advocate its use in social sci-ence research. Later action research is applied in the field of education, which is advocated by S. M. Corey, the head of the Horace-Mann-Lincoln Institute of School Experimentation at Columbia University in the 1950s. Since 1970s action research has been paid more and more attention by ELT researchers in European and American universities.

There are various definitions of action research in many forms according to different epistemologicalviews. However they have a core element among different definitions, which involves action research inquiring in one's own practice through a cyclical process that incorporates planning, acting, monitoring, re-flecting and re-planning. Action research and reflective teaching can be de-scribed as closely connected, but not same. Action research is the investigation of those craft knowledge values of teaching that exists in place when teachers are teaching. It concerns the transformation of research into action. As McFee (1993) shows that it is research into (1) a particular kind of practice-one in which there is a craft knowledge and (2) is research based on a particular model of knowledge and research with action as an outcome, this knowledge is surely practical knowledge.

The general cyclical stages of the action research process are described as plan (problem identification), research (literature review), observation (collecting data), reflection (analysis), and action (redefining the problem) according to the exploration in European and American universities. ELT teachers in European and American universities seek to investigate a problem (perceived or otherwise) and then start to plan how to investigate ways of solving this problem. ELT teachers start reading some background literature on the problem to give him/her ideas on how to solve the problem. Of course this research cycle will include talking to other colleagues about the concern as they may have some advice to offer. Then ELT teacher plan a strategy to collect data after the problem has been identified and researched. Once the data has been collected, ELT teachers will analyze and reflect on it and make a data-driven decision to take some actions. The final step in this spiraling cycle of research and action is problem redefinition. In this way ELT teachers can take more responsibility for decisions they make in their classes.

7 - 1 **Action Research Workshop**

7 - 2 **Improving by Action Research**

This sort of research essentially embodies the idea of reflective teaching in which ELT teachers conduct activities in the classroom and they may record a particular class or classes using audio or video records or just take a written account. Then they reflect on both the positive and negative aspects of that class. Next they take a proper action to improve the overall condition of classroom practice afterwards. It is always encouraging to implement action research in groups as one individual may not exert enough to notice all-important aspects of a particular class. If such a kind of research and reflection are carried on in a group mode, then it is possible for practitioners to collect all aspects of the classes that one individual fails to do.

Briefly speaking we can say that action research focus on understanding the teaching and learning situations, studying problems related to educational settings, developing the practitioners' proficiency and effectiveness that ultimately lead to learners' learning lessons. Hence, we may say that reflective teaching and action research serve the same purpose, i. e. improving ELT teachers' classroom practice. In addition the main responsibility for carrying out action research and deciding on courses of action research depends on the practitioners themselves. Therefore action research may often be conducted on self-finance mode i. e. practitioners themselves provide money for carrying on the research project in European and American universities. Moreover there is no requirement of a huge amount of money.

7.1.2 Action Research Model

Action research cycle can be listed and summarized in following seven steps according to Nunan (1992):

Step 1: Initiation: ELT teacher comes to the author with a problem: His current group of students do not seem interested or motivated in the class. What should be done?

Step 2: Preliminary Investigation: They spend some time collecting base-line data through observation and recording classroom interaction.

Step 3: Hypothesis: After reviewing the initial data, they form the hypothesis that students are unmotivated because the content of the classroom is not addressing the needs and interest of students.

Step 4: Intervention: ELT teacher devises a number of strategies for encouraging students to relate the content of the lessons o their own background and interest.

Step 5: Evaluation: After several weeks the class is recorded again. There is much greater involvement of students and complexity of their language and student-led interaction is enhanced.

Step 6: Dissemination: ELT teacher runs a workshop for his colleagues and presents a paper at a language conference.

Step 7: Follow-up: ELT teacher investigates alternative methods of motivating students.

From above-mentioned we come to see that action research owns a certain cycle which is called "Planning-Action-Monitoring-Reflection-Re-planning". It indicates that ELT teachers need to identify problems first to determine the solution and collect information. Then they will take actions. It refers to collect data while the class is going on through monitoring. ELT teachers will record the class or take notes to analyze important points in which they will reflect later. It requires researchers to think over the important observations regarding the classroom procedures. ELT practitioner-teachers will discard negative aspects of the class and promote some good aspects. Hence ELT practitioners can bring about a revolutionary change in their practice of English language teaching as well as education innovation in other fields.

7.1.3 Benefits from Action Research

Action research has no doubt brought immense benefit to ELT practitioners who are engaged in such a kind of project in any context. In some educational contexts where there is hardly any space and time for teacher training and teacher improvement, action research still prove to be the best way for teacher education and teacher development. Since no one can claim that, he or she knows everything or can apply all techniques appropriate to all classroom situations. Through sharing such experiences in real classroom situations, we can easily expect possible classroom behavior and make ELT teachers ready for dealing with all kinds of situations. Moreover a group of ELT teachers conduct action research, the whole teaching members can become fully prepared teachers to act towards the purpose. Thus action research can help ELT practitioners to improve their pedagogy. Concisely action research has many advantages in helping practitioners. It can improve professionalism among ELT teachers to make teachers more prepared; it is good to develop teachers' classroom effectiveness; it can also build up harmonious relationships between teachers and students; it also can ensure good teaching and learning environment to increase students' cognitive, social and constructive strategies for learning.

7.2 Present Situation in EFL Teachers' Professional Development

7.2.1 EFL Teachers' Professional Development

The concept of Continuous Professional Development (CPD) or Professional Development (PD) means that professionals continue developing themselves throughout their entire teaching profession instead of stopping developing once they start doing the job. To develop one professionally, both reflective teaching and action research can contribute significantly and these will help foster the idea of "Continuous Professional Development" (CPD) according to Roy Edwards (2010).

Roy (2010) explains continuous development as a systematic maintenance, improvement and broadening of knowledge and skill, and the development of personal qualities necessary for the execution of professional and technical duties throughout the working life. According to it, CPD is a life-long learning process. To quote Rubina Khan (2008), professional development includes a cluster of activities related to the enhancement of career growth and refinement of the skills of the practitioner. This is an all-inclusive definition of professional development. Khan also clarifies that professional development may range from activities like attending pre-service and in-service training to participating in conferences, seminars, workshops, joining teacher associations, reading books and articles etc.

To meet 21st century requirements, most educational projects expect ELT teachers to be able to catch up the latest academic and educational resources and have their own thoughts towards professional development as a lifelong learning process in order to be a successful teacher. It is well known that most ELT teachers are concerned about their personal professional development and consequences we can see that a large numbers of ELT teachers attend various professional development programs. To get the fruitful benefit of adopting professional development strategies, ELT teachers will have four types of awareness which are technical, personal, problematic and critical in European and American universities. Professional development is an ongoing process of learning by adopting multiple educational sources to ELT teachers to improve their performance during class, to maintain their competencies up to date and achieve the purposes in teaching/learning process successfully.

7 – 3 **ELT Teacher Training**

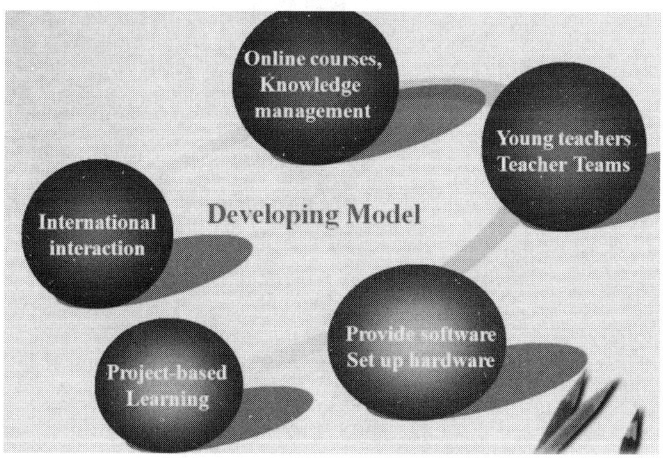

7 – 4 **Professional Developing Model**

Many ELT teachers are concerned about their professional development and hope that they can do better in the future during the class time. Nevertheless there are many difficulties during this process. Many teachers are reluctant to share others' problems and their good performances for the competition. The present situation both from abroad and China would be listed in order to stimulate ELT teachers do better in their professional development.

7.2.2 Current Situation abroad

Professional development has no fixed route and real end if it is viewed as lifelong learning and continues to work in the profession according to Rodrigues (2005). By using professional development resources and strategies ELT teachers will learn more about successful practices and implementation of instructional strategies and technology in their classrooms. In addition professional development has had to keep pace so as to provide ELT teachers with an opportunity to develop skills and experiences.

Moreover different strategies of professional development can help ELT teachers to understand the general cognitive and social/emotional characteristics of students. Those strategies give different techniques to tap the unique learning strengths of each student. Besides they may help ELT teachers to improve and use knowledge of their students' interests and backgrounds to assist them in planning meaningful and relevant lessons.

Patricia and Rhoton (2001) advised ELT teachers to consider five elements carefully in designing their professional development programs. These elements are:

(1) Determine self-goals and desired outcomes;

(2) Lay out a plan;

(3) Specify a time line for the plan;

(4) Reflect and evaluate each process;

(5) Make improvements.

It is clear that these elements emphasize designing professional development in strategic and thoughtful work. ELT teachers' education is simply a matter of offering what is easiest, most expedient, or most attractive method at the moment.

Banks et al (2001) classifies some areas for professional development to be considered by ELT teachers. These areas are:

(1) Subject knowledge and understanding;

(2) Development of teaching and assessment skills;

(3) Understanding teaching and learning;

(4) The wider curriculum and other changes affecting teaching;

(5) Management skills and managing people;

(6) Managing yourself and your professional development.

Despite the urgent need of ELT teachers' professional development, some obstacles constrict education strategies. These obstacles stop ELT teachers to practice different strategies of professional development and keep continual development.

Diaz-Maggioh (2004) anticipates some obstacles during teaching that ELT teachers may encounter. First it is the top-down decision making idea. It is easy for a teacher to consider decision from top to down, which means ELT teachers should make transpositonal consideration. Sometimes ELT teachers may also have certain concept that teachers need to be fixed, which is opposite to teachers' professional development. Teachers should conduct continuous learning during entire life. Teachers may also be lack of ownership of the professional development process and its results and the technocratic nature of professional development content would not benefit teachers' personal development. Sometimes they may think that there exists a universal application of classroom practices regardless of subject, student age, or cognitive development. Alternatively they may lack of variety in delivery modes of professional development, they just depend on one mode that is certainly not enough. During pursuing professional development they may not have enough opportunities. In fact self-learning becomes important and effective to communicate with other teachers and learn from teachers who have opportunities to pursue professional development. Moreover they may have little or no support in transferring professional development ideas to the classroom, which needs help from universities and government. Some may think that there are standardized approaches to professional development that disregard the varied needs and experiences of teachers. From long term view we have the same idea that teaching students may be in accordance of their aptitude however the standardized approach never exists. Some may also be lack of systematic evaluation of professional development. and have little or no acknowledgment of the learning characteristics of teachers among professional development planners.

Torff and Byrnes (2005) assess ELT teachers' beliefs about professional development initiatives. A scale for assessing ELT teachers' beliefs is developed and ELT researchers confirm reliability and validity. Results indicate that ELT teachers' attitudes about their professional development scale present scores with high reliability, which is a stable structure and satisfactory validity.

Baran and Cagiltay (2006) consider teachers' opinions on traditional professional development courses and their experiences from an online course. Based on presenting qualitative results and participating in an online professional development course they generally emphasize the lack of practice in both traditional and online courses. Further lack of theoretical concepts and contexts become their problems. They propose that ELT teachers' professional development (PD) programs should be promoted together by both academician and expert teachers.

Halim (2008) reveals the effect of a training program based on three professional development strategies, namely action learning, peer coaching and study group on improving teaching performance of the faculty of education in the light of pre-service standards for ELT teachers. The results shows that there are significant differences between the mean scores of the EFL teachers on the achievement test and the scoring rubric in favor of the post-test mean scores due to the effect of the professional development strategies.

Kesti (2008) proposes a conception of self-professional development for ELT teachers based on realization and contemporaneous trends. The results indicate that the concept of self-professional development is beneficial to 78.4% ELT teachers. According to their experiences, the practices of self-professional development used by ELT teachers are training programs in medium of reading books, journals and electronic publications however the barriers of self- professional development are class loading, abundant responsibilities, numerous students, absence of model lessons, training programs and workshops, lack of courage etc.

Atwan and Al-Faleet (2010) views the reality of self-professional development and its obstacles to ELT teachers. Their study results include that ELT teachers' practice of technology methods is 76% in self-professional development. They think that technological knowledge acquisition comes first in practice followed by participation in scientific events. According to their viewpoints administrative obstacles are much stronger than self-obstacles.

Granshaw (2010) also examines the nature and characteristics of effective professional development for ELT teachers. The conclusion of the interview data indicates that there is a wide range of characteristics which may be considered effective for ELT teachers, such as opportunity for them to work collaboratively in examining programs, student work, resources and exemplars. ELT teachers can build on their existing knowledge and skills which is most effective to them since the development of pedagogical content knowledge and subject content knowledge enables ELT teachers to construct new understandings of teaching and learning processes in technology education.

Actually the topic of teachers' professional development has won a widespread concern among ELT researchers. There have been some previous related studies in European and American universities. De Vries and Van de Grift (2013) investigated the relationship between teachers' continuing professional development (CPD) and their beliefs about learning and teaching in Dutch education context. A cluster of analysis produces three distinctive CPD profiles, reflecting relatively low, medium and high participation in CPD activities. The more teachers' participation in CPD, the more students will be oriented towards teachers. These findings can give us many implications to cultivate teachers' role in professional development and encourage their students to learning language better.

7.2.3 Current Situation in China

Although professional development is popular in European and American universities, current situation in china is not satisfying mainly in following reasons:

Firstly, ELT teachers in China are faced with great pressure in scientific research from teacher's perspective. On the one hand scientific research requirements for the discipline construction are put forward in recent years; on the other hand the scientific research environment of ELT teachers is also not reasonable, such as the lack of peer cooperation atmosphere, the lack of substantive content. ELT teachers are difficult to integrate into the scientific research team. Second ELT teachers have certain advantages in the relationship between teachers and students. ELT teachers attach enough importance to classroom teaching and teaching workload while the teaching curriculum is not stable and teaching evaluation is single in that lack of specific guidance and team collaboration is standing out. In particularly ELT teachers look forward to many more training programs, hoping that they have more opportunities for receiving training outside.

Secondly, ELT teachers in China are calling for university administrators to fully understand the present situation of language teachers and truly realize the healthy growth of language teachers for the long-term development from university management point of view. Through active guiding and intervention Chinese universities may promote teaching and scientific research cooperation among teachers, especially between new teachers and experienced teachers. Only through building cooperation can ELT teachers in China develop a constructive professional cooperation. Next schools or departments should further strengthen the cultural construction of teaching, namely scientific research team. They should pay more attention to cultivate new teachers and other teachers' professional development potential in the institution, and are committed to organize more participation of team members in substantial and active ways. Moreover they should take part in some organizations or activities in order to do better in stimulating ELT teachers into community instead of improving the soft environment of team development. At the same time suggestions on teaching and training will be given to ELT teachers so as to leave them more time and space to study and reflect.

Thirdly, ELT teachers in China think that the main factors that have impact on their personal professional development lie in heavy teaching burden since they have no training opportunities and lack of learning motivation. They do not know how to improve their teaching abilities. In fact there are different ways for ELT teachers to improve professional development, such as studying abroad, reducing workload to attend in-service training, studying in summer and winter vocation. Obviously ELT teachers' self-refection and action research will be most important. ELT teachers in China should undertake continuous professional development (CPD) to improve professional competency.

7.2.4 Different Ways of Pursuing Professional Development

From the above discussion we come to see that ELT teachers have strong expectation for self-professional development. Moreover here are two important methods to improve professional development, such as reflective teaching and action research.

(1) Reflective Teaching

Reflective teaching is beneficial to both pre-service and in-service teachers because it offers more advantages than disadvantages, teacher education programs are becoming more devoted to developing reflective practices in teaching context. These programs seek to help novice teachers become more aware of decision-making processes to help them make their decisions in context in which they are implemented. Therefore experiences before a "real job" will prepare ELT teachers for a better performance.

It is very encouraging to know that teaching education programs usually include extensive field practice before ELT teachers take full use of teaching responsibilities. These field practices help pre-service teachers to analyze different types of methodologies and strategies of teaching as they go along in their training. However it is important to pinpoint that reflective inquiry should start at this stage (training stage). It is valuable that pre-service ELT teachers can obtain from this self-inquiry as ELT teachers may share fresh ideas through analysis, synthesis, evaluation and reflection. These field practices can be discussed and solved on the spot by means of reflection-in-action and reflection-on-action process.

7 – 5 **Reflection-in-Action**

7 – 6 **Reflection-on-Action**

However how can this be done? Barlett (2000) have included a model of five elements in the cycle for the process of reflective thinking which in hand leads to professional growth to both pre-service and in-service ELT practitioners.

The model makes ELT teachers ask himself/herself questions such as "*What do I do as a teacher?*" in the mapping stage or preliminary stage to self-inquire as an individual and internally observing beliefs, attitudes, methodologies etc. In the second stage informing questions will be directed to the meaning of the teaching process itself, such as "*What did I intend?*". With the question ELT teachers deepens into what aims to determine successes or faults. When ELT practitioner ask him/herself questions like "*How did I come this way?*" or "*How was it possible for my present view to have emerged?*", then ELT teachers will step onto the stage which will oblige him/her to uncover situations and engage into discussions and reflection with colleagues by sharing ideas and thoughts. The fourth stage in this model deals with appraising, which is one of the most important stages because ELT teachers will inquire on new ways of teaching when he finds him/herself asking, "*How might I teach differently?*" During this stage there is a growth towards innovative actions to improve problems encountered in previous experiences. At last it is suggested that practitioners should experience an acting stage as an on-going stage of action where new ideas arise in a continuing process every time when the question is asked: "*What and how shall I teach now?*" This stage leads the reflective teachers to implementing new practice, observation, analysis and evaluation so as to determine if the implemented changes have worked or not. Reflection is central in all of the stages and professional growth. This process will force ELT teachers to step back and critically reflect not only on how they teach, but also why they teach in a particular way.

(2) Action Research

What is "action research"? We have discussed many aspects of action research. It is an effective way to improve teachers' professional development. Action research tends to be directly linked to achieving results in the classroom setting. The experimental dimension manifests that teachers' changes one thing and then observes effects of the change. This should lead to improvements in practice. Action research aims to lead ELT teachers become reflective or introspective on classroom practices. Such a teacher-as-researcher process is constantly reflecting on his/her practices, experimenting, evaluating the effects and then changing his/her practices if effects are positive.

Action research focuses on what works best with students in a particular setting. However it does not mean there is no "theory." It is well known that human beings engage themselves in theorizing every day. One way of looking at theory is to understand it as speculations about cause and effect that are backed by logic. Every time ELT teachers stop to think about why something has or has not happened, they engage themselves in theory making. There are expert theories, such as those by scholars like Einstein and Chomsky as well as theories of classroom practitioners. An example of ELT teachers' theory that could form the basis for action research is that calling on learners by name in class will cause them to participate more.

ELT teachers may find examples of expert theories on learner strategies based on experiments they have carried out. As classroom teachers ELT teachers are learners themselves, who are called "non-expert" theories. This is what action research guides ELT teachers focus on classroom teaching and take actions subsequently. The goal of action research, then, is to make ELT teachers aware of their own theories, which may be conscious or unconscious. It is awareness that leads ELT teachers to adjust their teaching behaviors to possibilities of change.

7.3 Action Research in ELT Teachers' Professional Development

Researching is a professional development activity that can be led by ELT teachers themselves or by institutes. Ferrance (2000) proposes action research aims at checking the effectiveness of already used or newly adopted teaching techniques. Solving practical classroom problems is another aim for action research in universities since it is practical rather than theoretical. Johnson (2011) states action research is an effective tool that university administrators can use to solve educational problems that do not have easy answers.

Action research assumes ELT teachers work better when thinking of a problem and it seeks a change in teachers' teaching practices based on research results. Action research includes questioning, gathering data, examining, investigating, changing results into actions, changing classroom environment and teaching practices. Therefore action research usually appears to solve a particular problem, and it is not about investigating why teachers use that particular strategy, but rather how they can improve and use that way better.

ELT teachers can conduct action research alone based on their classroom observation, or ELT teachers may work collaboratively. Collaborative action research includes at least two teachers or a group of teachers who have a classroom problem in common.

Hewitt and Little (2005) list a number of guidelines that ELT teachers should put into consideration before leading an action research. These are the following:

(1) Building knowledge of the action research process among teachers;

(2) Understanding the benefits of action research on learning output;

(3) Identifying implementation steps;

(4) Developing strategic goals that include action research for development;

(5) Establishing a support system for teachers;

(6) Providing professional development opportunities of action research;

(7) Provide opportunities for collaboration.

In evaluating a series of action research projects carried out by teachers in an immersion program in British Colombia, Lewis (1995) identifies three main payoffs:

(1) Through the process of systematically implementing their own choice of action project based on the needs of the students in particular, each teacher learned more about their own theories, or frames for teaching, and modified these frames to a certain extent.

(2) The frames for teaching of the participants in this study are related to the bigger questions of second language education and education in general. Practice cannot be understood thoroughly without appreciating how educational theory is expressed within teachers' frames and neither can theory be useful without recognizing that what counts is how theory becomes expressed within practice.

(3) Teacher as researcher or reflection in action approach to teacher education can be a very powerful way of facilitating change in the curriculum.

Most ELT teachers who have just graduated are probably experiencing the excitement and feeling of achievement from their graduation. However they should also be aware of that learning to be a teacher is "a life-long experience" from their first step (Crandall, 2001). The process of becoming an experienced teacher who is aware of his/her own philosophy of teaching and learning, who can efficiently draw on and adapt content knowledge, and who is capable of making decisions before, during and after every teaching and learning experience becomes more and more important. Professional development entails a constant search for answers to questions that arise from ever-new circumstances in educational contexts as time passes. The reason that questions emerge in this profession term after term, year after year is that, as Richards and Farrell (2005) explain, ELT teachers have changing needs at different times.

Professional development is a process of general growth that is not focused on a specific position but rather serves a long-term goal and seeks to facilitate growth of teachers' understanding of teaching and of themselves as teachers (Richards&Farrell, 2005), and is an activity that can be done by and for oneself (Wallace, 1991). Professional development usually takes place after finishing formal training for the purpose of keeping up to date with advancements in language teaching and research (Crandall, 2001).

Once in the context of the workplace, ELT teachers are responsible for their own development since they may not be as close to the sources of information as they are back at the language-teaching program. In response to it, there are a number of resources available to become better-informed language teaching professionals, such as (a) participating in professional language teaching associations, (b) subscribing to journals, (c) participating in electronic discussion groups, (d) making use of on-line teaching and learning resources, (e) working on institutional committees charged with curriculum or materials development, (f) working collaboratively with experienced colleagues, and (g) doing action research.

Among many resources, doing action research is an effective way for ELT teachers' professional development. Action research is smaller and more personal forms of inquiry, which can help ELT teachers' increase of their understanding on their own practices. The findings can be useful for improving any aspect of teaching and learning that they want or need, to focus on potential or perceived problems in classroom otherwise.

Even though the steps involved in carrying out action research are in essence the same for pre-service and for in-service teachers, the objectives and the applications of the findings differ to a degree. While pre-service teachers have the goal of preparing for future practice where they will be charged with more and more complex responsibilities than those in their practicum, in-service teachers may be analyzing familiar teaching and learning issues, which can be summarized in following cases:

(1) Identify an aspect of teaching, or one aspect of students' learning for research that is perceived as needing improvement;

(2) Deciding on the selection of a specific research method;

(3) Planning, designing and implementing data collection techniques and instruments;

(4) Planning and implementing an action plan for change;

(5) Evaluating any changes;

(6) Reporting results.

Action research should not be regarded as an activity conducted only by experts with specialized training who spend their time in laboratories. It needs to be seen as an extension of language teaching that all of us who work in language classrooms can carry out. Burns (1999) points out that action research is also participatory as it provides collaborative investigation in term of colleagues, practitioners and researchers, which can help teacher communities to resolve a greater number of teaching and learning issues.

To develop professionally, both reflective teaching and action research can contribute significantly and these will help foster the idea of "Continuous Professional Development". Therefore action research should become an effective way to promote ELT teachers' professional development.

Nunan (1992) provides a checklist, which is adapted from Cohen and

Manion (1985) for action research projects:

(1) Identify a problem and it is important that the problem be narrow and focused.

(2) Develop a plan to carry out the research, discussing and negotiating with other teachers, advisors and outside experts.

(3) Review at least some of what has already been written about the issue in question.

(4) Restate the problem in the form of a hypothesis or research question; discuss the assumptions underlying the research project.

(5) Select research procedures, materials, resources etc.

(6) Choose the best way to evaluate your results.

(7) Collect data, analyze it, and evaluate your project.

(8) Interpret the data and feed the information and insights back into your own teaching and to others, perhaps in the form of a workshop or a written report.

There is different understanding about action research but Nunan (1992) definition encapsulates the major elements for ELT teachers, he states that action research is a form of self-reflective inquiry carried out by practitioners, aimed at solving problems, improving practice, or enhancing understanding. It is often collaborative. It involves four cyclical or spiral stages of planning, acting, observing and reflecting in general which is widely accepted by ELT teachers in European and American teachers.

Action research enables ELT teachers to try new ideas with a minimum of risk, it makes the task of bringing about manageable change by forcing them to make improvements step by step, it allows them to introduce changes gradually so that they are almost imperceptible to others in the environment, who might otherwise be unsympathetic, and it allows ELT teachers to involve others in the change process. It is the need for language teachers to feel safe while they attempt to explain another strategic reason for choosing such an approach in the programs and assessment task.

Those who use action research discover that it is an evolving process and, as one question is answered, another question arises. At first this approach to research was problematic for the participants because they are expected to find, and be assessed on the perfect answer. Alternatively there is no perfect solution, and any chosen solution creates problems of its own, which is part of participants' growing awareness, and contribute to the maintenance, sustainability and evolution of their professional development. The analysis of the submitted action research project reports shows how all the participants find new problems and directions because of their action search projects.

New insights are innovative so that ELT teachers need to be more active in each class and give clearer instructions, or develop new texts for their students. Such reflective responses indicate that the completed action research projects have their desired effect on the post-course learning and continue to make changes that they previously thought impossible.

Action research techniques used and taught in the programs require ELT teachers to think about ways to improve their language teaching. Action research requires the participants to plan for the improvements they identify, implement these improvements, observe what happens, reflect on their observations and then re-plan. ELT teachers will give specific action research procedures in the form of case studies as far as possible, which is specifically related to participants' EFL teaching contexts. Once participants are familiar with action research procedures, they may identify and clarify their own language teaching needs. The participants are assisted to make plans that develop solutions to meet these needs. The participants will implemented their plans since the use of this approach is one way that the concepts are developed in the sustained programs after the participants have completed action research assessment tasks. Anyhow the analysis will be confirmed that action research approaches, teaching methodologies and techniques introduced in the course are modified and implemented in ways that are relevant to the participants in their teaching contexts.

Usually the submitted tasks will demonstrate an encouraging uptake of the main content of the programs. ELT teachers will identify relevant methodological issues such as how to increase learner-to-learner interactions, how to increase talking time and how to teach grammar communicatively.

More importantly in terms of sustainability, the submitted action research projects show ELT teachers are willing to use action research approaches for future development of language teaching skills. It is noted that they can find new problems to solve because of completing their preliminary action research task. This indicates that ELT teachers have developed a disciplined means of taking action, exploring and reflecting on results as significant skills in language teaching.

Many ELT participants demonstrate that they are professionally more confident in attempting methodological changes, and more creative in their approaches to these changes. A number of the ELT participants ask colleagues to observe their classes for the purposes of inspection and professional assessment while others develop their own language teaching materials and shape an awareness that their learners need to be active members in the class so that classroom power can and should be shared for the benefit of the learning process.

Hence there is one typical example from the action research summaries in more depth to illustrate the social-constructivist concepts of the maintenance of learning used in the programs and to demonstrate the value of action research to effect change. Then ELT participants are concerned on their awareness of the necessity for their learners to be engaged interactively in language learning and of providing opportunities for his learners to practice their second language. In order to address these puzzles, ELT teachers plan to try a number of activities and approaches and use warm-up in his classes to achieve following effects:

(1) Give all learners an equal chance to talk;

(2) Reduce the amount of immediate teacher feedback;

(3) Organize class presentations and activities more coherently;

(4) Encourage and motivate the learners;

(5) Allow the learners more thinking time for responses.

ELT teachers initiate actions to fulfill his plan and survey the learners to ascertain their learning styles. They will organize more pair and group work, and allow learners to rearrange the usually fixed seating arrangements. Simultaneously they allow more learners thinking time and ask his colleagues to observe his classes to record and compare the amount of student talk to teacher talk. After implementing these actions, they observe that their learners appear more active, motivated and engaged in the lessons. Consequently the learners will understood more about the language and concepts being taught. It is noted, however, that the new techniques require him to prepare and plan better. Through their reflection, re-planning and observations, ELT teachers are more able to select suitable exercises, activities and tasks. Naturally they learn how to arrange their teaching profiles more effectively to maximize students' motivation.

The most encouraging outcome is that his plans for the future include, not only using and sustaining the learning outcomes of the program they have attended, but also sharing his new approaches to problem solving. In the process they plan to organize and implement a professional development program where he would report on their action research project, and promote its use among colleagues. ELT teachers also plan to apply the methods of action research to attempt to solve new classroom puzzles that emerge during reflections, such as gaining access to alternative texts for learner use, and development of a bank of classroom activities.

Some typical examples show that ELT teachers could make changes, introduce new techniques, implement new methodologies, develop an institutionally professional development program for colleagues and become more creative and confident within professional context. This participant would not have believed that such incremental changes were possible until he had actually completed them. Other action research reports show that the methodological research include the management of large, mixed-ability classes, quality and quantity of learner-to-learner interactions in the target language, the introduction of communicative techniques and the development and maintenance of learner motivation.

The summary of the action research projects indicates that varieties of new teaching techniques are used, self-observed, or observed by colleagues. The reflection and re-planning aspect of the projects indicate that new methodological concerns stimulate learning emerge because of continuous professional development (CPD).

More than half OF the respondents state that they will continue to benefit from action research approaches. This again indicates that ELT teachers can be empowered to enhance their teaching approaches even within the confines of restrictive EFL curricula, if they are given the tools to do so, and if they are given the required practice in using these tools.

7.4 Bridging Gap between Theory and Practice

ELT Teachers around the world have different views about whether theory is more important than practice or vice versa. Some people would argue that teachers must possess rich background knowledge in order to be able to teach effectively while others would claim that theory does not guarantee a good performance that knowledge is acquired by practice. Both arguments are valid. The key to effective teaching is definitely a balance between theory and practice. Collin (1996) ever claimed that some in order to be able to teach effectively practitioners are skeptical about the value of theory and question its relevance, mainly because they do not how to use it. We come to see that theory is important not only to perform well, but also to be able to answer students' questions. For example, ELT teachers need to know about language acquisition theory to be able to explain students' behavior and help them in the learning process. At the same time theorists need to be exposed to have first-hand experience in which to base or apply in their research. Dahlin (1996) proposes following statements that teachers need to demonstrate their research base by conducting their own classrooms research (reflective practice) and by reading, using, and citing professional journals. The time has passed when teachers can simply say 'It works.' They have to show that they understand the hows and whys of theory and practice.

Imel (1992) suggests ways for understanding these hows and whys:

(1) Questioning what, why and how one does things and asking what, why, and how others do things;

(2) Keeping an open mind;

(3) Comparing and contrasting;

(4) Seeking the framework, theoretical basis, and underlying rationale;

(5) Viewing from various perspectives;

(6) Asking for others' ideas and viewpoints;

(7) Using prescriptive models only when adapted to the situation;

(8) Considering consequences;

(9) Hypothesizing;

(10) Synthesizing and testing;

(11) Seeking, identifying and resolving problems.

Indeed these strategies or processes will help ELT teachers reveal any type of discrepancy between theory and practice. It will also bridge the gap among educators who tend to implement teaching practices without understanding why, and those who know why certain types of teaching practices should be implemented but do not know how. That is why two different types of educators are found in higher education settings: those with a vast expertise on theory and research practices, but with difficulties in teaching practices; and those novice professionals who can implement innovative and wonderful activities, but with little understanding about the rationale behind their teaching practices. Both types of professionals are missing one of the two components, theory and/or practice. Beyer (1984) has explained that situations like this (gap between theory and practice) occur because there is a tendency "*to accept existing classroom situations as given, essentially unalterable, and beyond criticism*". He believes that once this happens, critical thinking or any other alternative possibility is considered useless or irrelevant. Therefore many close-minded educators are reluctant to change. Perhaps the key to avoid this taken-for-granted attitude is to prepare ELT teachers for the possible situations they will encounter and train them with teaching tools so that they can deal with these problems before they enter the classrooms. I believe that if both pre-service and in-service teachers are aware of the benefits of reflection, and if they experience the potential of this process, the results would be overwhelming as it would narrow the gap between theory and learning and would ensure more effective and self-confident instructors in the field of ELT teaching. Richert (2010) highlights this in the following statements:

The ability to think about what one does and why - assessing past actions, current situations, and intended outcomes - is vital to intelligent practice, practice that is reflective rather than routine. As the time in the teaching process when teachers stop to think about their work and make sense of it, reflection influences how one grows as a professional by influencing how successfully one is able to learn from one's experience.

In sum linking theory and practice through research inquiry brings flexibility in instructional settings by helping practitioners examine successes and failures in a constructive environment and promote self-awareness and knowledge through personal experience. It also provides practicality because it not only asks practitioners to make connections between their beliefs and what really is happening in different contexts, but also involves those types of practitioners who teach in varied contexts and meet a great range of individuals with different styles of learning. Thus opportunities to explore and reflect on techniques, ideas and approaches are considered in the research process and immediate links between theory and practice are established. Added to this, linking theory and practice brings professionalism as a matter of promoting deliberate actions in planning, and as a way of implementing instructions and ongoing engagement with theory by assessing, revising and implementing new theories and practices. It also provides sustainability since time is allotted for reflection, implementation and follow-up practices.

Action research requires a commitment, a commitment towards change, towards understanding, and most importantly, a commitment towards continuous self-development. If practitioners are willing to invest time, effort and resources in this type of training, action research can indeed be an effective means for professional growth.

In China, theory and practice influence each other and are influenced by each other's development. As Eraut (2011) indicates:

Not only is an idea reinterpreted during use, but also it may even need to be used before it can acquire any significant meaning for the user. Thus, its meaning is likely to have been strongly influenced by previous contexts of use; and the idea will not be transferable to a new context without further intellectual efforts.

In order to promote Chinese EFL teaching and learning, many advanced theories of education which are developed in European and American universities have been introduced in the new national curriculum, such as Communicative Language Teaching (CLT), TBLT, and learner-center and so on. These concepts, however, are always criticized by teachers for their lack of practicality. For example, as Wen and Xue (2005) point out, although some advanced foreign theories from European and American universities are introduced to Chinese EFL teaching and learning, the refusal to acknowledge the local context divorces the theory from practice. Chinese EFL teachers also try to promote students' autonomous learning by adopting experiential teaching in the context of Chinese traditional receptive learning. Moreover they finally argue for critical acceptance of foreign theories and critical incorporation of traditional concepts in EFL teaching and learning. More concerns about practicality have been raised in relation to theories. Common issues have been addressed by many researchers, such as inappropriate levels of difficulty with respect to tasks for students at different linguistic and cognitive levels, teachers' lack of pedagogical knowledge in conducting ELT teaching, and the neglect of grammar presentation in carrying out tasks.

The gap between the principles and practices of learner-centeredness are discussed for years. We believe that as learner-centeredness is more of an ideology than a specific set of classroom procedures or techniques, many ELT teachers do not know what exactly they should do in the classroom to realize learner-centeredness. Some ELT teachers are found to equate a class that is fun for students with learner-centeredness. This may result in their teaching being enjoyable but having a tendency to downplay the language to be learned. In this case, it is important to empower Chinese ELT teachers to relate the abstract concepts with their classroom practice.

There are more emphasis that has been laid on the use of EFL teaching approaches and methods, which are creatively and flexibly based on Chinese teachers' own judgment, experience and beliefs. Studies of ELT teachers' cognition make teachers to fully understand discrepancies between theoretical recommendations based on researches and classroom practice, and moreover such studies attempt to explain the lack of influence on practice of educational innovation. Besides the study of ELT teachers' cognition can employ more teachers in a form of reflective learning by making them notice the psychological bases of their classroom practice, which can help them understand their mental lives, but does not dictate practice to them. In this circumstance converting theory into practice can be established by constructing theory in teaching practice. It is our personal belief that Chinese EFL teachers should be supported to link theory with practice in adequate context so as to accelerate Chinese EFL teacher education.

Bibliography

[1] Atwan, A. and Al-Faleet, G. The Reality of Professional Development and its Obstacles among Technology Teachers in Gaza Governorates Schools. Educational Technology and Technological Education Conference, Al-Aqsa University, October, 2010: 195 –220.

[2] Banks, F. et al. Teacher early Professional Development: the Context of Early Professional Development for Teachers. Frank Banks and Ann Shelton Mayes (editors) Typesetters, Cambridge, 2001.

[3] Baran, B&Cagiltay, K. The Turkish Online Journal of Distance Education. Turkey-DOAJ Teachers' Experiences in Online Professional Development Environment, Anadolu University, Eskisehir, Volume7, Issue 4, 2006: 110 –122.

[4] Bartlett, L. Teacher Development through Reflective Teaching. New York: Cambridge University Press, 2000.

[5] Burns, A. Collaborative Action Research for Language Teachers. New York: Cambridge University Press, 1999.

[6] Brown, D. Teaching by Principles: An Interactive Approach to Language Pedagogy. New York: Addison Wesley, 2001.

[7] Beyer, L. Field Experience, Ideology and the Development of Critical Reflectivity. Journal of Teaching for Education, 35 (3), 1984: 36 –41.

[8] Crandall, J. Keeping Up to Date as an ESL or EFL Professional. In Celce-Murcia, M. Ed., Teaching English as a Second or Foreign Language.

Boston: Heinle&Heinle, 2001.

[9] Cohen, L. and L. Manion. Research Methods in Education. London: Croom Helm, 1985.

[10] Colllin, A. Re-thinking the Relationship between Theory and Practice: Practitioners as Map Readers. British Journal of Guidance and Counseling, 24 (1), 1996: 67.

[11] Diaz-Maggioli, G. Teacher-centered Professional Development. ASCD: United Sates, 2004.

[12] De Vries, S&van de Grif, J. Profiling Teachers' Continuing Professional Development and the Relation with their Beliefs about Learning and Teaching. Teaching and Teacher Education, Elsevier, Volume33, 2013: 78 -89.

[13] Dahlin, A. The Teacher as a Reflective Professional. College Teaching, 42 (4), 1996: 57 -60.

[14] Edwards, Roy. Teachers as Action Researchers. Modern English Teacher. 19 (2), 2010.

[15] Eraut, M. Developing Professional Knowledge and Competence, London: Falmer, 2011.

[16] Ferrance, E. Action Research. Themes in Education, 18 (3), 2000.

[17] Florez, M. C. Reflective Practice in Adult ESL Settings. ERIC Digest, No. 135, 2004.

[18] Freeman, D. The Hidden Side of the Work: Teacher Knowledge and Learning to Teach, Language Teaching, 35 (1), 2002: 1 -13.

[19] Granshaw, B. How Does Development Support and Improve Practice? Victoria University of Wellington, Research Masters Thesis, Retrieved May 30th 2013 from http: //hdl. handle. net/10063/1582.

[20] Halim, S. M. The Effect of Using Some Professional Development Strategies on Improving the Teaching Performance of English Language Student-Teacher at the Faculty of Education, Helwan University in the Light of Pre-service Teacher Standards. Unpublished Ph D, Helwan University: Faculty of Education, 2008.

[21] Hong, L. Research on TBLT in EFL Teaching in the Context of Curriculum Reform. New Curriculum Research, 132 (12), 2008: 44 -45.

[22] Hewitt, M. A., and Little, M. Leading Action Research in Schools. State ofFlorida, Department of Education, 2005: 1 – 30.

[23] Imel, S. Reflective Practice in Adult Education. ERIC Digest, No. 12, 1992.

[24] Johnson, C. School Administrators and the Importance of Utilizing Action Research. International Journal of Humanities and Social Science, 14 (1), 2011: 78 – 84.

[25] Khan, R. Developing Professionally. The Dhaka University Journal of Linguistics, Vol. 2, 2008.

[26] Kesti, L. Suggested Conception of Self Professional Development for English Language Teachers of girls public schools Based on Realization and Contemporaneous Trends Unpublished Dissertation, Umm Al-Qura University Faculty of Education, 2008.

[27] Kemmis, S., & McTaggart, R. (Eds.). The Action Researcher Planner (3rd ed.). Geelong, Australia: Deakin University Press, 1998.

[28] Lewis, C. A little off balance: Exploring teachers' experiences with a new curriculum in French as a second language through teacher inquiry. Burnaby, British Columbia, Canada: Simon Fraser University, 1995.

[29] McFee, G. Reflections on the Nature of Action-research. Cambridge Journal of Education 23 (2), 1993: 173 – 183.

[30] Nunan, D. Research Methods in Language Learning, Cambridge University Press, 1992.

[31] Nunan, D. Designing Tasks for the Communicative Classroom. Cambridge: Cambridge University Press, 1989.

[32] Patricia, F. B. and Rhoton, J. Issues in Science Education: Professional Development: Planning and Design. NSTA: The United States of America, 2001.

[33] Rodrigues, S. Model of Teacher Professional Development: The Partnership in Primary Science Project. Nova Science Publishers, Inc: Hauppauge, 2005.

[34] Rodrigues, S. Teacher Professional Development in Science Education. International Perspectives on Teacher Professional Development, Ro-

drigues, S. (editor) Nova Science Publishers, Inc. 2005: 1 – 13.

[35] Richards, J. C. &Farrell, T. S. C. Reflective Teaching in Second Language Classrooms. Cambridge: Cambridge University Press, 2005.

[36] Richardson, V. The Evolution of Reflective Teaching and Teacher Education. R. T. Clift, W, R. Houston &M. C. Pugach (Eds.), Encouraging Reflective Practice in Education. New York: Teachers College Press, 1990.

[37] Richards, J. C. and Rodgers, T. S. Approaches and Methods in Language Teaching, Cambridge: Cambridge University Press, 2010.

[38] Stringer, E. T. Action Research: A Hand Book for Practitioners. Newbury Park: Sage, 1999.

[39] Torff, B.; Sessions, D. and Byrnes, K. Assessment of Teachers' Attitudes about Professional Development. Educational and Psychological Measurement, Vol. 65/No. 5, October 2005: 820 – 830.

[40] Wallace, M. Training Foreign Language Teaches: A Reflective Approach. Cambridge: Cambridge University Press, 1991.

[41] Wen, X., and Xue, G. Reflections on Some Problems of Basic Education in the Curriculum Reform. Curriculum, Teaching Material and Method, 25 (8), 2005: 11 – 17.

[42] Yang, Y. and Wen, Q. On Task-based Language Teaching. China Adult Education, 24 (1), 2007: 148 – 149.

[43] Wang, Y. and Li, L. A Tentative Analysis on the Five Fundamental Issues of English Education. Curriculum, Teaching Material and Method, 27 (2), 2007: 55 – 58.

注　　解

1. 教师专业化发展（TPD，Teachers' Professional Development）：教师专业化发展是指教师作为专业人员，在专业思想、专业知识、专业能力等方面不断发展和完善的过程，即从专业新手到专家型教师的过程。首先它表现为教师专业发展的多样性，高校历来就是更新知识、创造知识的基地，教师除承载着为社会源源不断的输出人才之外，还担负着专业领域内的科研工作。教师工作的复杂性决定了教师专业发展的多样性；其次它表现为教师专业发展的自主性，由于近年来高校改革对教师队伍的高要求，教师的学历水平普遍较高，并且高校作为知识更新与创新的发源地，教师较易接触教育及学术的发展前沿，促使教师不断自主学习，主动参与各种途径的学习培训，不断促进自身专业发展；再就是教师专业发展的持续性，一方面教师专业发展是一个持续不断的循序渐进的动态过程，另一方面教师专业发展贯穿于教师的整个职业生涯。

2. 专业能力持续发展（CPD，Continuous Professional Development）：这里指的是大学英语语言教师终身发展及提高其专业知识的手段以及英语语言教师不断完善其知识结构所需的技能及实践经验，它可以是一种正式的或非正式的自主学探究性学习。

3. 反思教学实践（Reflective Teaching）：反思（Reflection）是教师以自己的教学活动为思考对象对自己所作出的行为、决策以及由此所产生的结果进行审视和分析的过程，它是一种通过提高参与者的自我察觉水平来促进专业能力发展的途径，同时也是对教学经验的反思，又称反思性实践（Reflective Practice），同时它也是一种经验思考问题的方式，要求教师具有做出理性选择并对这些选择承担责任的能力，即“经验 + 反思 = 成长”的过程，没有反思的教学经验是狭隘的经验，至多只能形成肤浅的知识，如果大学英语教师仅仅满足于获得经验而不对经验进行深入的思考，那么其发展将大大受到限制。

4. 大卫·努南（David Nunan）：大卫·努南博士 1949 年 10 月 11 日生于澳大利亚布罗肯希尔，他是世界上最大的英语语言教学组织 TESOL（Teaching English to Speakers of Other Languages）的前任主席和 ELT 系列教材作者，他的英语教育系列教材“Go For It!’在全球总销售总额超过 2.5 亿。2000 年大卫·努南曾担任世界上最大的语言教学协会 TESOL 的主席，曾先后在澳大利亚、英国、美国、泰国、日本、新加坡、中国香港和拉美国家任教和从事研究，他对 ELT 的许多见解至今仍然在欧美大学广为应用。